GIVING CHRISTIANITY BACK TO AGAPE LOVE

A New Paradigm for Being Church Together

MATTHEW CARRIKER

LifeRich Publishing is a registered trademark of The Reader's Digest Association, Inc.

LifeRich Publishing books may be ordered through booksellers or by contacting:

LifeRich Publishing
1663 Liberty Drive
Bloomington, IN 47403
www.liferichpublishing.com
844-686-9607

Because of the dynamic nature of the Internet, any web addresses or links contained in this book may have changed since publication and may no longer be valid. The views expressed in this work are solely those of the author and do not necessarily reflect the views of the publisher, and the publisher hereby disclaims any responsibility for them.

Any people depicted in stock imagery provided by Getty Images are models, and such images are being used for illustrative purposes only. Certain stock imagery © Getty Images.

All Scripture quotations are taken from New Revised Standard Version Bible, copyright © 1989 National Council of the Churches of Christ in the United States of America. Used by permission. All rights reserved worldwide.

ISBN: 978-1-4897-2639-1 (sc)
ISBN: 978-1-4897-2640-7 (e)

Print information available on the last page.

LifeRich Publishing rev. date: 05/05/2022

CONTENTS

The Cover Art to this book is by my mother, Lynn Carriker.

As she describes:
In this photo of the Ocean waves, the colors I chose meld into each other:
Blue representing both the heavenly realms and the sea. Blue also speaks of depth, trust, wisdom, faith, freedom, sincerity.
Green speaking to nature/ Mother Earth, growth, renewal, rebirth.
White- purity, illumination, brilliance.
Ocean- a representation of the Creator's ongoing, evolutionary, dynamic nature. Form into formlessness, unfathomable, mystery, Life, constancy.
The waves have formed an open heart in the center where Love can flow.

FOREWORD BY MIRABAI DEVI

I am grateful to Rev. Matt Carriker for writing this book, meant to dispel the many dogmatic, fear-based belief systems, myths and misinterpretations that have arisen over time in the name of God and Jesus. Many of these beliefs have caused a greater divide of separation than we could have ever imagined. This book serves to dispel these illusions and false "truths," providing a solid understanding grounded in the deep wisdom of what was intended to be the true messages and teachings of Christ.

Matt closes this gap, illuminating a pathway that takes us back to the heart and to unconditional love, setting us free.

I cannot think of a better person than Rev. Matt Carriker to write this book. Matt has studied Eastern yogic teachings while practicing meditation for many years, along with his interfaith work and being an ordained Christian minister. Matt has had direct inner contact with God/the Divine in his own internal chamber of the heart for a very long time, and has studied with some of the greatest Spiritual Teachers and Masters in the world. I have had the privilege of knowing Rev. Matt Carriker and guiding him in interfaith spiritual training and Mentorship for 15 years, and I can attest to his spiritual maturity, devotion to God, and integrity.

Matt has experienced that all the Masters come from the same space, even if the religions or outward appearances are different. Matt reminds us that "Giving Christianity Back to Agape Love" is always focused on the same thing- love, compassion, peace, forgiveness, and serving one another. That is what Jesus was about. That is the Agape, unconditional love Jesus pointed us towards. And that is Matt's deep desire in writing this book- that the religion in Jesus' name return to the people, as they deserve to know the true heart of God's Love, which is without conditions or limitations, and which is equally in your heart as it is in mine. Thank you Matt for the gift of this book, so that all of us might return to that heart of unconditional love in our religious beliefs, our spiritual practices, and in our lives.

I recommend that you share this book with everyone that you know that is dedicated to the spiritual path and is ready to receive a deeper level of embodied wisdom, truth, understanding and spiritual awakening.

Yours in Service to the Divine,
Mirabai Devi

INTRODUCTION

Christians have a love-hate relationship with the church.

There are many reasons why Christians love the church. Church was the place that Christians grew up in; a place that nurtured us spiritually as a child or an adult; a place where we developed relationships with mentors and friends that fed us spiritually. Most of all, church was the place where Christians found the unconditional and freeing love of Jesus.

Jesus, the head of the church, sets a very high standard of love. In every age, saints have been true to Jesus' life and message, infusing new life, meaning, and purpose into the church. Yet most Christians in any age are just normal people. They try to live their lives as best they can (and in the time they have) according to the life and faith that Jesus modeled and taught. In every time of history, Christians have fallen short of Jesus' standard of love.

This is where the love-hate part comes in.

When Christians "miss the mark", you hear stories like those of Derrick and Kat, who were kicked out of their church after questioning core "Christian" beliefs. You hear stories like those of Jason and Joy, who were wounded by churches that condemned their sexual identity and turned them away. You hear countless stories of people who have experienced judgment, condemnation, or limiting beliefs in Jesus' name, and so turned away from the church in disgust.

When people see non-loving actions within church walls, they often describe the church with one word: hypocritical. "Jesus might be a cool guy, but I don't see much of him in the church that I've experienced."

How could a church that has been plagued by anti-Semitism, the killing of the Crusades, and the violence of the Inquisition (just to name a few) be redeemed of these evils? Quite simply, it has always returned to Jesus. When you return to Jesus, you return to the heart of his message: agape. Agape is a Greek word in the New Testament referring to a love that is without limits and beyond conditions. Agape is the love that God has for us, and that we are called to have towards one another.

In a time when churches are dying and failing, giving Christianity back to agape love has the power to bring life into a religion that feels old, worn out, and over-institutionalized. To return Christianity to Jesus is to give the church universal back to a love that is boundless, free, and unconditional; to a love that finds its heart in service, peacemaking, and radical transformation; to a love that will set the world on fire.

An unofficial subtitle of this book could be "My Handbook for Progressive Christian Faith." I say "My" because no two Christians, let alone two "progressive" Christians, believe the same thing. The well-known saying, "Ask two Jews, get three opinions" is true for Christians as well. We do not all believe the same thing. Some Christians who identify as "progressive" will strongly disagree with my beliefs.

Nevertheless, part of being "progressive" is openness to the process of dialogue- listening with an open heart, even when others disagree with you; committing to respectful conversation where we truly hear the other side, acknowledging and honoring the perspective of another. To be "progressive" spiritually is seeking to progress to a place where we see God in every person, even those whom we have negative feelings towards. You may not agree with all the words on these pages. That's okay. I invite you into dialogue-with me, and most importantly, with yourself. Let these words open you to your own highest thoughts and deepest wisdom- to the wellspring of God within you. Blessings on the journey.

CHAPTER ONE

AGAPE: UNCONDITIONAL LOVE

There's a story Jesus tells in the fifteenth chapter of Luke's gospel, often referred to as the parable of the "Prodigal Son." Jesus' parables were not "true" in that they factually happened. They were "true" in that they point to a deeper spiritual truth that we are invited to live out.

The parable of the Prodigal Son points to the truth of agape love.

In the world we live in, conditional love is the norm. Loving relationships with friends or romances are entered into unconsciously as a trade agreement. What can this person give to me? What will I get in return for being with this person? The unconscious but unstated rule is, "If this person gives me acceptance, I will give them acceptance."

The trouble with trade agreements happens when one party doesn't hold their side of the bargain. Then the entire relationship falls apart. A breach of trust in relationship calls for the withholding of love or service.

Agape love can be found in families, in romance, and in friendship, but agape love is beyond familial love, beyond romantic love, and beyond the love we experience in friendship. Agape is a love without conditions. Agape is the first love that each of us are loved with. Agape, divine love, is who we are at our core. "We love because God first loved us."[1]

---

[1]   1 John 4: 19, New Revised Standard Version

According to our cultural story, the father in Luke's parable should have rejected his wandering, prodigal son. The son hadn't lived into his side of the bargain. The son had dishonored his father and taken his share of the inheritance.

Hadn't the son wasted his father's hard-earned money? The only "fair" solution on the father's part would have been to tell his son: "Sorry. You had your chance."

Agape love, however, isn't fair. Divine love isn't something that we "deserve" or earn. The radical thing about divine love is this-God loves us, and there's NOTHING we can do about it. In the words of Philip Yancey, there's nothing we can do to make God love us more, and nothing we can do to make God love us less.

This is the love embodied by the father in Luke's story. Rather than scold or disown his younger son, the father welcomes him back with open arms. Jesus points us to this love again and again and invites us to live our daily lives from that place.

If you don't see yourself reflected in the disobedient rebellious younger son, you might resonate with the older son. The elder son worked faithfully for his father for years. He had never disobeyed his father. Isn't it unfair that the father had never thrown so much as a party for the faithful, obedient son? Isn't the older son's resentment justified?

Agape is never embodied through jealousy or resentment. The Apostle Paul captures this in his letter to the Corinthian community:

"If I speak in the tongues of mortals and of angels, but do not have love, I am a noisy gong or a clanging cymbal. And if I have prophetic powers, and understand all mysteries and all knowledge, and if I have all faith, so as to remove mountains, but do not have love, I am nothing. If I give away all my possessions, and if I hand over my body so that I may boast, but do not have love, I gain nothing.

Love is patient; love is kind; love is not envious or boastful or arrogant or rude. It does not insist on its own way; it is not irritable or resentful; it does not rejoice in wrongdoing, but rejoices in the truth. It bears all things, believes all things, hopes all things, endures all things."[2]

Many of us associate fairness with justice. If that was true, God's love for us would be based on what we "do." The better we do, in other words, the more God will love us.

Conversely, if we just believe the right thing, God will find favor with us.

The image of God as a Judge, sitting on a throne, judging good and bad, is what many churchgoers grew up with. This Judge determines our merits based on whether we've met the correct standard of belief or behavior. This Santa Claus god rewards or punishes us according to whether we've been "naughty" or "nice."

From this view, God's love of us is based on whether or not we've measured up. If we measure up, God rewards us with heaven. If we don't, God punishes us with hell and damnation.

Ironically, this image is the opposite of the God that Jesus presents and models for us in scripture.

My knowing that God loves us unconditionally is based not only on Jesus' teachings, but from the experiences of my own life. One of the most formative spiritual experiences impacting the direction of my life happened not to me, but to my mother.

April 17, 1979, the day that I was born, changed my parents' lives, and my life, forever. That is because on the day that I was born, my mom had a near death experience, though she isn't sure if she ever clinically died. Thankfully, my mother is alive today, and raised me and my two older siblings into adulthood.

In April 1979, my mother had never heard about Near Death Experiences (NDEs). Most people hadn't. And so, my mother had no frame of reference for what was to happen to her next.

In my mother's own words:

---

[2]   1 Corinthians 13: 1-6, New Revised Standard Version (NRSV); note: all subsequent biblical references will be from the NRSV unless specifically noted.

"At the time of your birth, I breached. The situation became urgent when my heartbeat started dropping. After giving birth, I began to hemorrhage, and was losing lots of blood. At that point, I found myself floating above myself and watching the Doctor and staff working on me. I felt myself leave my body. I could see my body, the room, the lights, the anesthesiologist, and everyone else in the room who was working on me. I traveled towards the hallway where dad was working on the bench. I felt my spirit melt into him with so much love. I felt my spirit leave him, and then I was floating as if in a mist.

"All of a sudden, there was an incredible presence of someone's spirit. It felt like this was an incredible spirit of someone, perhaps Christ, or even a divine being. In the presence of this spirit, I felt so much love, and so much peace. Then I felt myself leaving the spirit, and I was rushed to an incredible light. I was overcome by the presence of the Great Presence, the one I call God- but who answers to any name. The Holiest of Holies surrounded me with so much love that to this day just the thought of this love brings me to my knees in gratitude and humility. It was so incredibly powerful, more than words could ever describe. It felt like love, and like joy, and yet no words could ever describe it.

"As I was being bathed in this incredible love I began thinking of all those things I had done in this life which were not good or kind or loving; that were selfish and reckless and thoughtless. I felt like saying to God 'You don't want to love me this much, cause I've done a lot of bad things.' But there was no judgment, only more love; unconditional, exquisite, extravagant, limitless love. At some point I could feel myself moving from this Presence and feeling such excitement to tell Eric and my children, my friends that GOD IS REAL, GOD IS BEAUTIFUL- that there is only LOVE and Grace and it never ends."

Though God is often associated with a vengeful, wrathful, Judge, that is not the God that Jesus revealed or that my mother experienced. Jesus did not present a God who was the arbiter of the

Ultimate, Divine Trade Agreement- "Do or believe the right things, and you'll receive my love. If you don't, you won't!"

This is us creating God in the image of human love!

Thankfully, I had a mother that not only experienced God's unconditional love but was a pure channel for that love in the world, and in my life.

God's unconditional love has the power to heal our broken world. It is this love that we are called to live out and embody in our own lives. This love is good news for a world hurting and plagued by violence and fear.

The journey of faith is our response to God's agape love. Albeit imperfectly, we are called to live into Jesus' great invitation- to love God with all our heart, soul, mind and strength, and to love our neighbor as we love ourselves. (Matthew 22: 37-39)

The rest of this book centers around this one assumption: God loves us unconditionally. Our task- individually and as communities- is to be instruments of that love.

CHAPTER TWO

EMBODIMENT

As a youth, I grew up as many people in the mainline Christian church do- being confirmed, going to youth group activities, and then, falling away from church for a bit.

Yet growing up, there was one experience in church that kept me engaged and inspired. That experience was an annual work camp to West Virginia.

Though my first trip to the West Virginia work camp was to fulfill my high school's requirement of thirty community service hours, I was pleasantly surprised by the unexpected experiences I had. During work camp, I met and connected with young people from all around the country. I was touched by levels of devotion, service, and love that I had never seen before in community. Feeling inspired by my work camp experience, I travelled down to Appalachia every summer in high school to make homes warm, safe, and dry.

When I got to college, I drifted from church a bit. Weekly college parties became more regular for me than church attendance. Surprisingly, during this new college trend, I continued travelling to work camp every June during summer break.

Every year, work camp would close with a special Friday night worship service. Work campers would stand up and share how they had been touched by the people they met, the families they served, and the work they had done. The founder of the work camp would give an inspiring message, and the entire community would break bread together. At the end of the service, we would hold hands around the pavilion and sing "We Are One in the Spirit."

This worship service was always both joyous yet sad. By Friday night, everyone had completed their work site, finished their Bible study group meetings, and was preparing to head home the next morning.

One summer at this closing Friday worship, I felt more reflective than usual. I was already missing work camp: the community, the feeling of fulfillment, the great love that was shared. In my sadness, I remember thinking to myself: "What if, at the end of work camp, we were invited to stay? To do this work year-round. Would I stay? Would I do it?"

I didn't know my answer to that question, but the possibility of saying "yes" excited me. Amid a rebellious college stage, the West Virginia work camp provided much needed purpose at a time when I was hungering for something deeper and more meaningful.

During my college years, the inspiration I found at work camp ultimately led me to say "Yes" to new, more meaningful possibilities. By the end of my senior year in college, I had chosen to go abroad and serve as a Jesuit Volunteer for two years in Belize. As I left college, spirituality was taking an increasingly more important role in my life.

≪✼≫

Now, more than 20 years after college, I understand why the West Virginia work camp touched my life so deeply. Work camp was an embodiment of all that I saw as good, true, and beautiful in Christianity. The people at work camp "embodied" a faith that was lived out- a faith that modeled in so many ways the essential teachings of Jesus. As a community, the West Virginia work camp embodied love to a degree that I had never experienced before.

In the simplest sense, that is my reason for writing this book. I see a deep need to give Christianity back to a faith that is embodied and lived out. A faith that isn't lived out has little power in a world where faith is also used as a weapon. As the letter of James puts it: "Faith by itself, if it has no works, is dead."[3]

In our contemporary culture, many people have left church altogether because they don't see within its walls a faith accompanied by works. If they do see a faith accompanied by works, too often that faith that seems colored by judgment and hypocrisy. A recent Washington Post article stated: "Majorities of young people in America describe modern-day Christianity as judgmental, hypocritical and anti-gay. What's more, many Christians don't even want to call themselves "Christian" because of the baggage that accompanies the label."[4]

Though the church has seen saints, mystics, and great teachers throughout its history, the life of Jesus' followers is usually not so idyllic. At best, critics of the church say that it lacks inspiration and wisdom. At worst, many cite instances where the church has inflicted harm, or been a source of judgment or exclusion. In a recent conversation, a Pastor colleague remarked to me half-jokingly: "You know, church would be great... if it wasn't for the people."

Pastor Molly Phinney Baskette affirms that though Christianity is a religion of transformation, "many expressions of Christianity have been, especially in the last century, watered down, defanged, co-opted by the machinery of capitalism, and distorted by human ambition...The Catholic Church is one of the wealthiest and most powerful corporations in the world- and Pope Francis has met with extreme resistance from even those in his own ranks, who prefer

---

[3] James 2: 17, New Revised Standard Version
[4] http://www.usatoday.com/news/religion/2007-10-10-christians-young_N.htm

custom-made Prada vestments to feeding the poor. It's no wonder we have made Christianity un-believable."[5]

Given this state of affairs, what can we do about Christianity today? What can we do about the massive hoards leaving church? What is our response to the judgment, harm, and violence too often done in Jesus' name?

I find my answer in the one key word: embodiment. Jesus' life was a life of deep and profound embodiment- of the fruits of the spirit, of service, of compassion in action. For Christians, and for people of every spiritual tradition, Jesus' life is a source of constant inspiration and wisdom. Jesus' embodiment of a life lived in love, peace, joy, and God-centeredness is unparalleled in my experience.

Though Christians preach love, peace, and joy, our actions and beliefs too frequently tell a different story.

A wise proverb says: "Your actions speak so loud; I can't hear what you're saying." Jesus followers too often forget that words mean little when they are not embodied in our actions. Words become "incarnational" through our actions. Our words take on a living, breathing, physical reality through our deeds.

The heart of "Giving Christianity Back to Agape Love" is embodiment and incarnation. "Giving Christianity Back to Love" is not about converting people from other religions to Christianity or judging those who have fallen short of the highest standards of love. "Giving Christianity Back to Love" is about embodying all that Jesus embodied; about living and "incarnating" all that Jesus lived and incarnated.

As was the case with the disciples, embodying also means shedding. This shedding might be compared to a cup full of old, rotting vegetables. If you want to fill that cup with new, fresh vegetables, you've first got to get rid of the old ones.

---

[5] Phinney Baskette, Molly, *Standing Naked Before God: The Art of Public Confession*, (Cleveland, The Pilgrim Press, 2015), 14-15.

Most of us know what Christianity needs to shed. It needs to shed its judgment of others; its condemnation of people of other faiths, and of no faith at all. It needs to shed its attachment to dogma and limiting beliefs that no longer resonate with common sense Christians- beliefs about salvation and sin, God and Jesus, scripture, science, and sexuality. Christianity needs to shed the ways that violence and prejudice are perpetrated in the name of God, religion, and Jesus. It needs to shed its idea that Christians have an exclusive hold on spiritual truth, thus perpetuating religious superiority in our pluralistic world.

Numerous Christian beliefs, attitudes, and actions are sucking life out of the church today. What Christianity needs is a breath of fresh air and new life. Christianity needs the original power, passion, and love of the one who started it all: Jesus.

Here is one in whom we find not judgment, but agape, unconditional love. Here is one whose compassion never contracts but is ever expansive. Here is one who invites us to reach out in service and make peace in our world. Here is one whose teachings and life we can look to and trust.

Yes, the life of this one has the power to infuse new life into an increasingly jaded and stale religion. Jesus invites us to die to old ways to make room for resurrection and new life; to make room for a spirituality that inspires us anew each day in living out the fruits of the spirit- love, peace, joy, patience, kindness, generosity, faithfulness, gentleness, and self-control.[6]

---

[6]   Galatians 5: 22-23, New Revised Standard Version

CHAPTER THREE

A NEW CHRISTIAN REFORMATION: BELIEFS AND EMBODIMENT

Though Massachusetts (the state where I live) is not a very religious place, a high percentage of people in this area consider themselves spiritual. Demographics show that people in Boston and Waltham (the city where I serve as Pastor) aren't so interested in attending church services, whereas interest in yoga, mindfulness, spirituality retreats and service opportunities has spiked.

A lot of traditional church people I know are grieving this reality. "Where are the people- the young ones especially?" "Why have they stopped coming?"

Mainline churches across the United States are mourning this decline, for which there are many reasons. With the loss of anything that is important to us, including the loss of church as we have known it, grief is an important and necessary step. Our grief honors the love and appreciation we have for church traditions and experiences that have shaped us.

For religious people, it is important to grieve not only the loss of church as we have known it, but also the great harms that have been perpetrated in the name of religion. As a follower of Jesus, I grieve deeply the hurts to countless people done in the name of Christ.

A surface glance at history shows how entrenched the church has been in anti-Semitism, the subjugation of women, and the rejection of persons who are lesbian, gay, bisexual, transgender, or gender non-conforming. A quick historical study shows the oppressive violence of the church towards people considered "heathen," "pagan," or "heretics," which includes Muslims, Native Americans, "witches," atheists, and anyone considered non-Christian.

The church is complicit in what Jim Wallis calls "America's original sin- the theft of land from Indigenous people who were either killed or removed and the enslavement of millions of Africans who became America's greatest economic resource."[7]

For centuries, Christian circles have been defined by theological beliefs rooted in a vengeful, violent, judgmental God. These beliefs have been the foundation for vengeful, violent, and judgmental Christian behaviors. It is no wonder that people aren't interested in church. Modern people resonate with Gandhi's statement, "I like your Christ. I do not like your Christians. Your Christians are so unlike your Christ."

The current perception of Christian culture and communities is so toxic that most young people outside the church think of Christians as judgmental, hypocritical, anti-gay, and out-of-touch with reality.[8] Overall, most people see Christianity as a set of outdated beliefs. And they're not wrong. So, we grieve.

Yet, an increasingly vocal minority in the church is seeking a different way. This minority mourns the fear and violence committed in the name of Jesus, while seeking to move the church in a radically different direction. In this new direction, love comes first, and beliefs are secondary. "Are we ready to say that Christianity must no longer

---

[7]   Wallis, Jim, *America's Original Sin: Racism, White Privilege, and the Bridge to a New America*, (Grand Rapids, Brazos Press, 2016), 9.

[8]   http://www.usatoday.com/news/religion/2007-10-10-christians-young_N.htm

be defined by a list of unchanging beliefs, but rather… by a way of life centered in love, as embodied by Jesus?"[9]

A consistent thread in Jesus' life is his persecution at the hands of the religious elite for challenging laws, traditions, and beliefs that weren't in alignment with love. Jesus was considered a heretic in his day for asserting the supremacy of love. Prophetic Christians today are simply saying that we never fully got or lived his message in our church communities.

Jesus' life and ministry weren't about ushering in a new set of beliefs. Early followers of Jesus were known as "The Way." Albeit imperfectly, those early disciples sought to live out the path of love that Jesus embodied and taught them: "By this everyone will know that you are my disciples, if you love one another." (John 13: 35)

In short, Jesus offered a new way of holding our beliefs, based on one criterion- love.

In the gospels, Jesus respects the law and beliefs, except when they no longer resonate with, you got it, love.

Jesus' question to Christians today is simple- do your beliefs align with love?

This question calls Christians towards deep self-reflection and examination. If we are known as Jesus' disciples by our love, not by our beliefs, then we must take a long and close look at how we re-orient our lives and our communities.

Jesus came to bring in the age of love. The early church was on fire for divine, unconditional, inclusive love. Imperfect though this early church was, those disciples and communities were so magnetic because they lived out a way of love and grace, even when it meant persecution and martyrdom.

Most of Jesus' difficult words were directed at religious authorities whose beliefs acted as a barrier to love. Several hundred years later

[9] McLaren, Brian, *The Great Spiritual Migration: How the World's Largest Religion is Seeking a Better Way to be Christian*, (New York, Convergent, 2016), 48.

in the era of Constantine, Christianity on the whole reverted back towards a foundation of beliefs.

It is perhaps the ultimate irony that beliefs again became primary, now in Jesus' name. Since the 4th century C.E., it has been a vocal minority of mystics, prophets and peacemakers that have seen the path of Jesus first and foremost as the path of love. This vocal minority is increasing.

Our current reformation in religion does not negate the importance of beliefs. Indeed, our beliefs influence and determine our behavior. Modern day mystics and reformers are encouraging us to move back to a simpler creed: that love is our path, love is our guide, and love is our foundation.

In this spirit, we ask of any belief, ritual, or tradition- does it align with love? Let's test it and find out. Can we be as unforgiving with traditional Christian beliefs as scientists are with their hypotheses? Most every other discipline in human history has change and evolution built into it. Yet theology has been resistant to this trend.

The hordes of people voting with their feet about church are proof enough that this trend is no longer tenable. Scholars, theologians, Pastors, mystics, and religious leaders from all walks of life- we must begin the difficult task of examining and evaluating our faith. As we do, we will find that there is much to leave behind. This is the "rummage sale" Christianity must undergo to survive as a religion. It is a much-needed purification of unhelpful religiosity, so that the spiritual depth of Jesus' life and ministry can emerge once again.

As people of faith, we "do not grieve as others who have no hope."[10] And this is the good news- underneath all the rubble and grief, there is something beautiful, powerful, and largely untapped. It is the witness of "The Way." It is the embodiment of unconditional love, service, and peace that we see manifested in Jesus' life, teaching,

---

[10]   Dorhauer, John, *Beyond Resistance: The Institutional Church Meets the Postmodern World*, (Chicago, Exploration Press, 2015), 48.

and ministry. It is the life that Jesus lived, and that he calls us to in his parables and teachings.

We will have to sift through a lot of bad news before the good news can emerge. We will have to grieve the old as we usher in the new. But we do not grieve without hope. This is the story of the church- death and resurrection; the old passing away, while something new is being born. We have fallen short, but God's love and faithfulness remain constant. Our task is simple, but not easy- to be instruments of that love today.

☙ ❧

How important are our beliefs? It's interesting to see what Jesus thought about beliefs.

In his parable of the Good Samaritan, Jesus makes it clear that the righteous one is not the Pharisee, or the lawyer, both of whom are learned and know about the law and "correct" belief. The righteous one in the parable is the one who cares for his neighbor and reaches out to the stranger in need.

Jesus' harshest words were for the religious authorities who knew all about proper doctrine, dogma, and traditions, but didn't embody the spirit of the law. Jesus' toughest words were for those strong in the knowledge/letter of the law, but who didn't live the essence of the law: Love.

For Jesus, belief wasn't as important as it was to live in such a way that the Kingdom of God comes to earth. Proper doctrine wasn't as essential as it was to live one's life in compassionate service through humility, peacemaking, and love.

When we get too legalistic about religious things, religion becomes a stumbling block for others. Then people think the whole of religion is about belief.

People today are turned off even from the word "Christian" because it is so fully associated with belief and doctrine. In many churches, belief is used as a spiritual gatekeeper- determining whether you are Christian or not; whether you can be part of a church community or not.

Jesus' attitude was starkly in contrast to spiritual gatekeeping. When Jesus called his first disciples, he didn't summon them over to recite the Torah verse by verse. Jesus said simply "Follow me." And the first disciples followed. For Jesus, a willingness to follow in the way of discipleship and risky love was more important than intellectual knowledge or beliefs.

❧ ☙

While beliefs are not the foundation of our faith, our beliefs are important. The beliefs we hold determine the behaviors we live out. In other words, beliefs create behaviors.

"All behaviors are sponsored by beliefs. You cannot make a long-term change in behaviors without addressing the beliefs that underlie them."[11]

Jesus questioned beliefs that were out of alignment with love. Being Jewish, Jesus observed Shabbat, the taking of a Sabbath day of rest. When beliefs about Sabbath got twisted from their original intention, Jesus challenged them. Jesus wasn't concerned with the letter of the law as much as with the spirit of the law- whether beliefs and actions led towards or away from love.

Today, beliefs shared in the name of Jesus are turning thinking people away from church. Beliefs seen as "Christian" do not resonate with the God of agape love that Jesus incarnated. Here are two examples that will be addressed more in later chapters:

First, the belief that homosexuality is a sin. This belief has led to the treatment of non-heterosexuals as sub-human. It has led to the basic human rights of LGBTQIA individuals being denied, and to LGBTQIA individuals not being welcomed as full participants (just as they are) into communities of faith.

---

[11]   Walsch, Neale Donald, *The New Revelations, A Conversation with God*, (New York, Atria Books, 2002), 16.

Second, the belief that God created only one right way home through Jesus Christ. According to this widely held doctrine, any person subscribing to a belief system or religion different from Christianity is condemned for eternity. As a result of this doctrine, the primary Christian approach to relationships with people of other faiths (or of no faith) is through a lens of conversion.

One of my faithful friends recently joked that many Christians have a "warm heart, but chilly theology." This is the disconnect that many people feel within church, me included. Many times, I have visited a congregation and been warmly welcomed by church members. As time passes, however, a disconnect is evident between the warmth of the people and the theology they hold dear: "The people are kind, but the God I hear about does not seem like a deity I would want to follow."

Christians are generally kind-hearted, but their beliefs often tell a different story- a story of a God who is NOT kind. It is this "chilly theology," of a God who favors some and rejects others, which has turned hoards away from the church.

I know many Christians for whom this tension has become a real spiritual crisis. These Christians love the church and the people within it. However, they simply can't wrap their minds around the theology presented to them.

It is a mistake to think that theology and beliefs are not important. Our ideas about who God is and what Life is influence how we live and interact in the world. If we are made in the image and likeness of God, then what image of God are we following?

Christian theologies have too often created a God in our own image: a divine being who loves us conditionally, as we tend to do in our human relationships. Yet as Yvette Flunder says, "Any theology that suggests that God receives some and rejects others is not reflective of the ministry of Jesus Christ."[12]

---

[12]   Flunder, Yvette: *Where the Edge Gathers: Building a Community of Radical Inclusion*, (Cleveland, The Pilgrim Press, 2005), p. 7.

What if our task, as a church, was to reconnect to the God of unconditional love? To do so, we must examine the beliefs that Christians have used in creating a God in humanity's image. To give Christianity back to agape love, we must shed old beliefs and traditions that do not align with unconditional love.

If God loves us without conditions, boundaries, and limitations, then our task, being made in God's image, is to do the same.

Knowing that religious beliefs have been used to hurt, exclude, and judge others, Jesus' invitation for us is to value love over belief. Knowing that Jesus had strong words for those who clung too tightly to their beliefs and traditions, we would do well not to claim that we hold THE universal truth.

As we affirm that "God is Still Speaking", we do well to hold our beliefs lightly, knowing that wisdom and new revelations are constantly springing forth from God's well of abundant life.

Humility theology recognizes that we are workers, not master builders, ministers, not Messiahs. We do not possess all spiritual answers for eternity. Faith is not so much about certainty with our answers, as it is faithfulness to the questions. As Rainer Maria Rilke said over a century ago in "Letters to a Young Poet": "Have patience with everything unresolved in your heart and to try to love the questions themselves as if they were locked rooms or books written in a very foreign language… The point is to live everything. Live the questions now. Perhaps then, someday far in the future, you will gradually, without even noticing it, live your way into the answer."

CHAPTER FOUR

ONENESS

Of all Jesus' teachings that Christians have not lived out, neglect of Oneness stands out above the rest. Oneness is at the core of Jesus' life and message. Disregard for Oneness has turned away masses from church and resulted in severely damaging effects on people outside of church.

In the gospel of John, Jesus prays "that they may all be one." (John 17: 21) What does it mean for us to be "one?" What does "Oneness" look like?

Oneness does not actually "look like" anything, for it is not something we see, feel, hear, taste, smell or observe with our physical senses. Paradoxically, the metaphor of the body is an apt one for understanding Oneness.

When we look at the body, various parts appear separate. Underneath what we can see, however, separateness is an illusion. The illusion of separateness "is created by identifying too strongly with the external."[13]

Connection is the opposite of separation and is at the heart of Oneness. In Oneness, every part of the body is connected to every other part: "the head bone's connected to the neck bone... the neck

---

[13]   Moorjani, Anita, *Dying To Be Me: My Journey From Cancer, To Near Death, to True Healing*, (New York City, Hay House, 2012), 144.

bone's connected to the shoulder bone…" Though body parts appear separate with our senses, at a deeper level they are all connected.

Oneness also means interdependence. Every body part is *connected* to every other body part and *interdependent* on all other parts. What happens to one body part- be it a relaxing massage or a traumatic injury- isn't isolated but affects the whole body. Paul, the first century Christian apostle, said that we are "one body." Affirming the body's connection and interdependence, Paul stated, "If one member (of the body) suffers, all suffer together with it; if one member is honored, all rejoice together with it." (1 Corinthians 12: 26)

৵৽

During his lifetime, Jesus invited all who would hear to live within the "kingdom of God." In the Christian tradition, this kingdom of God is spoken of paradoxically as "already" and "not yet." "Already" means that the kingdom is *here now*, among us ("the kingdom of God has come near"- Mark 1: 15). "Not yet" means that the kingdom is not yet fully realized. We have our part to do in bringing about the kingdom of God, and that part is not yet complete. We are reminded of this every time we pray the Lord's Prayer, "Thy Kingdom come, thy will be done, on earth as it is in heaven."

Oneness is synonymous with what Jesus called "the kingdom of God."

In places filled with violence, hatred, and judgment, Christians work to bring about the kingdom of God ("Oneness") by spreading peace, love, and understanding. In places where unnecessary poverty, disease, and hunger are found, Christians work for the "coming of the kingdom" by spreading opportunity, health, and security.

Remembering each side of the "Oneness" coin is essential. On the one hand, we are "already" one. I am one with you; you are one with me. We are one with all of creation, and with God.

At the same time, we haven't fully grasped or lived out Oneness. "Thy kingdom come."

Increasing amounts of people are waking up to the reality that "we are all One", but billions have not. Oneness is already, and simultaneously not yet.

Being already "one," every action we take has an impact on those around us, depending on its intention and "energy." When we are kind, our kindness impacts others in an uplifting way. When we are unkind, our thoughts, words, and actions impact those around us in a downward-pulling way.

Being mean impacts not only the receiver of unkindness, but also the giver.

The brain wonderfully illustrates how this occurs. When the chemical serotonin is released from the brain, it produces positive feelings in the body of peace, happiness, and harmony. When we receive kindness, our serotonin levels increase. When we give out kindness, our serotonin levels also increase. Even more fascinating, merely *witnessing* kindness has the effect of increasing our serotonin levels!

Similarly, when we smile, our brain releases the neurochemical dopamine, "which improves *your* mood and your reality as well."[14]

Separateness is the illusion. Our actions impact not only others *and* ourselves, but the *entire world* around us!

Have you ever been unkind to a loved one, only later to feel sadness and regret? Have you ever given compassion to a friend in need, or been generous to a stranger, and suddenly felt a lot better? The *Conversations with God* books put it this way: "What you do to another, you do for you, and what you fail to do for another, you fail to do for you."[15]

---

[14]   Achor, Shawn, *before happiness: the 5 hidden keys to achieving success, spreading happiness, and sustaining positive change*, (New York, Crown Business, 2013), 195.

[15]   Walsch, Neale Donald: *The New Revelations: A Conversation with God*, (New York, Atria Books, 2002), 280.

There's a part of the brain that isn't time or object oriented, and so doesn't distinguish between giving and receiving. In other words, when I give love out to another, a part of my brain doesn't distinguish between whether I'm giving or receiving love. In a very real way, I receive what I give. What I do to another, I do to myself.

Our small actions impact the world at large. A small change in one area can be the catalyst for an even greater change in another area. The term "butterfly effect" states that "if a butterfly flaps its wings in Tokyo, then a month later it may cause a hurricane in Brazil."[16]

In our global, technological world, actions on the part of one country instantaneously have ripple effects on other countries. Wise countries know that international relations are crucial to national security. Quite obviously, the impact of nuclear weapons in far off countries (Iran, North Korea, etc.) are not contained or isolated to those countries alone.

Counter to Oneness is the old theological paradigm of separation. In the separation paradigm, each of us lives our life without concern for what others are doing. "You live your life, I'll live mine." With a separation foundation, interdependence is lost in favor of independence; connection misplaced in favor of individuality.

Increasingly, we are waking up from the illusion of separateness, realizing that our actions towards each other and the earth can no longer be taken without consequence. Many awakening people ask the obvious, practical question: "Given that we're one, but aren't fully living out Oneness, what steps can we take?"

Jesus' path to Oneness begins with the "Golden Rule." Masters of all spiritual traditions have affirmed this "Golden Rule" as a path towards Oneness. Expressed by Jesus in Matthew 7:12, these words

---

[16] Braden, Gregg: *The Divine Matrix: Bridging Time, Space, Miracles, and Belief*, (New York City, Hay House, Inc., 2007), 93.

invite us: "In everything do to others as you would have them do to you; for this is the law and the prophets."

Today many secular and spiritual leaders are encouraging us to act from the "Platinum rule:" to treat others as they would want to be treated.

Both the Golden and Platinum Rules invite us to step out of our shoes for a moment and imagine ourselves in another's reality. As we prefer to not be judged, these words ask us not to mete out judgment. As we don't want others to condemn us, this "rule" asks us not to condemn others. As we hope others forgive our mistakes, we are invited to forgive others.

All of us want our basic needs of health and security supplied for. This rule invites us to work in supplying those necessities for others.

Jesus responds to those who come to him with compassion, not judgment. He invites us to do the same. In the gospel of Matthew, Jesus articulates a vision of Oneness and the kingdom of God where we live out the Golden Rule through compassion and service:

> "Come, you that are blessed by my Father, inherit
> the kingdom prepared for you from the foundation
> of the world; for I was hungry and you gave me
> food, I was thirsty and you gave me something to
> drink, I was a stranger and you welcomed me, I was
> naked and you gave me clothing, I was sick and you
> took care of me, I was in prison and you visited me."
> (Matthew 25: 34-36)

Lest we become so religious that we neglect the needy in our midst, Jesus reminds us that so long as children are hungry, he is hungry. Mother Teresa, serving the poorest of the poor in India, expressed how she saw the face of Christ "in all of his distressing disguises."

The Millennium Development Goals articulated by the United Nations are one basic starting point for the Golden Rule. These eight

Millennium Development Goals, (MDGs) express Oneness and the Golden Rule by:

1. Eradicating extreme poverty and hunger
2. Achieving universal primary education
3. Promoting gender equality and empowering women
4. Reducing Child Mortality
5. Improving Maternal Health
6. Combating HIV/AIDS, malaria, and other diseases
7. Ensuring environmental sustainability
8. Developing a global partnership for development

These goals are not an exhaustive list, but an essential starting point.

Entering a life of service means coming face to face with the devastation that many people prefer to avoid. Seeing this "not yet" side of Oneness- hunger, poverty, premature death, division, an earth at risk- can easily lead to overwhelm and despair.

Such feelings are not only normal, but the sign of a healthy conscience. To be sad that thousands of people die every day from hunger related diseases shows that our heart is still beating. We must allow ourselves to feel our feelings. This is an essential starting point in not succumbing to "tragedy fatigue." Even the people who have most positively impacted the world regularly feel feelings of despair and overwhelm.

Our feelings can paralyze us, or they can be a catalyst for action. In the words of Edward Everett Hale,

"I am only one.

But still I am one.

I cannot do everything, but still I can do something.

And because I cannot do everything, I will not refuse to do the something that I can do."

In working towards Oneness, we cannot take every step overnight. In the NOW we can only take the step in front of us. "The journey of a thousand miles" says Lao Tzu, "begins with a single step."

At the heart of Giving Christianity Back to Agape Love are everyday small acts of kindness. The world may not change overnight. Our job, paradoxically, is not first to change the world. Our job is to change ourselves first by being instruments of God's love and Oneness in our lives and relationships. Our job is to practice giving without attachment to the fruits of our actions. Our job is to not get so caught up in the magnitude of our tasks that we give up or burn out.

There is joy on the journey, as Jesus reminds us: "I have said these things to you so that my joy may be in you, and that your joy may be complete." (John 15:11) In the spirit of Jesus, let us embody the joy, peace and love we wish to see as we work towards making God's Kingdom of Oneness real in the world.

CHAPTER FIVE

ORIGINAL BLESSING, ORIGINAL SIN

Our answers to the foundational spiritual questions "Who is God?" "Who is Jesus?" and "Who am I?" shape our beliefs, and in turn our behaviors. It is important to think carefully about these questions, because for centuries traditional Christian answers have been rooted in fear, not love.

The primordial human question, "Who am I?" has long been answered in churches out of a theology of fear, rather than the experience of love.

Just like with Oneness and the kingdom of God, humans have what may seem like an identity paradox. This paradox is that the kingdom of God inside of us is both "already" and "not yet."

What are we already? We are love. We are goodness. We are peace. We are wonderfully, beautifully made in the image of unconditional love. That is our intrinsic birthright which nothing can change. Being human means living into who we already are, made in God's image of love.

As humans, we have fallen into what might be called "spiritual amnesia." This is the "not yet" piece. We don't remember who we are, and consequently, who others are (being all interconnected in Spirit). This spiritual amnesia means that we often treat ourselves, others, and the earth with less than loving-kindness. We have forgotten our original birthright. Therefore spiritual teachers speak of faith as a journey of "waking up."

Though humans are both "already" and "not yet," Christianity has almost exclusively emphasized our "not-yetness," or put another way, sin. As a result of this focus, we too often forget our unchangeable identity as beloved children of God. This identity is who we already are. Nothing we DO can take away from that identity.

Contrast this with the "original sin" doctrine started by Augustine. This doctrine is founded in a belief in "the fall," rooted in Genesis chapter 3. At the beginning of Genesis, Adam and Eve live harmoniously with God in the Garden of Eden. The serpent tempts the first humans to eat fruit from the tree of the knowledge of good and evil, which God has ordered them not to eat from. After disobediently eating fruit from this tree, God expels Adam and Eve from the Garden.

According to Christian tradition, humans were subsequently condemned to a life of struggle, guilt, sin, and mortality, in contrast to the ease, innocence, and immortality they had once known in paradise.

Christian interpretation of this scripture suggests that Adam and Eve's act of disobedience had eternal implications. While the first man and woman began from a state of innocent obedience to God, their choices doomed humans to a state of guilty disobedience.

Thus the "fall" brought sin into the world, corrupting human nature. As a result, all humans are born into this state of "original sin."

So pervasive is this teaching that even today many Christians have a fear of babies dying before being baptized. This fear is rooted in the belief that the unbaptized child will be condemned to eternal damnation or purgatory.

Matthew Fox, author of "Original Blessing," writes "What a difference it makes to teach our children that they are blessings first and 'sinners' only second. So much low self-esteem, internalized oppression, and violence to self and others rule our society forcing bouts and binges of addictions ranging from bulimia to consumerism."[17]

For centuries, Christianity has perpetuated the belief that humans are born in sin.

While we do sin, sin is not the whole of who we are. An exclusive religious focus on sin has produced unparalleled emotional repression and sexual dysfunction in society.

Sin, which we might define as "missing the mark," does exist in our world. In differing spiritual traditions, it is known by different names: dukkha, illusion, maya, or ego. We cannot deny that if our primary goal in this earth is to love, humans are missing the mark, and have been missing the mark time and again. Something inside humans causes us to act perpetually from fear and violence, even when we don't want to. As the apostle Paul says in his letter to the Romans, "I do not understand my own actions. For I do not do what I want, but I do the very thing I hate. I can will what is right, but I cannot do it. For I do not do the good I want, but the evil I do not want is what I do." (Romans 7: 15, 18-19)

Sin is not an inevitable reality and our ultimate destiny, but it is the reality that we humans have imitated, learned, and repeated throughout history. If we read the scriptures metaphorically, we could say that the first act of Adam and Eve (or the first fear-based human act) was original sin because it brought sin into the world, causing it to multiply. After Adam and Eve, violence begins to spiral out of control through the actions of Cain and subsequent generations.

It is human nature to act out what we see and learn from our own experience. As more fear and violence have entered our world, this negative spiraling effect has become increasingly harder to stop.

And yet, the "original sin" of humans is nowhere mentioned in Genesis, in the Hebrew Bible, or in the New Testament. Sin has

---

[17]   Fox, Matthew, *Original Blessing*, (New York, Jeremy P. Tarcher/Putnam, 1983), 4-5.

come into the world, but nowhere do the scriptures say that we are inherently sinful. That "original sin" is a new dogma sparked by Augustine is evident in that no such notion exists in Judaism or other earlier spiritual traditions.

What Christians have lost sight of is our "original blessing." In the account of the creation of the world, God brings all things into being and calls them good. On the sixth day, creation comes to completion in humanity: "Let us make humankind in our image, according to our likeness... So God created humankind in his image, in the image of God he created them; male and female he created them. God blessed them... God saw everything that he had made, and indeed, it was very good." (Genesis 1: 26-28, 31)

The Genesis text says that we are made in God's image and likeness. God blesses us and calls us "very good." Nowhere in Genesis or elsewhere in scripture does it say that this original blessing is retracted; nowhere does it say that we are no longer "very good." To lose sight of our original blessing is to lose sight of who we are, and of who our Creator is.

Jesus points to this original blessing in his teachings and parables. Jesus does not say that we are born in sin, but rather that we are "the light of the world" and "the salt of the earth." At the same time, Jesus is aware of the destructiveness of sin. He admits that we hide our light under a bushel, preventing it from being seen. When we forget our original blessing, Jesus says that we become as salt that has lost its flavor. (Matthew 5: 13-16)

As spiritual beings made in the image and likeness of God, our task is to wake up to our true, ever-existing, untouched identity. Sin, fear, and violence have crept into the world, covering over our true nature. No matter how hidden, our spiritual nature continually invites us to "wake up." The prophets throughout the Bible, Jesus included, invite us to awaken. "The Kingdom of God is at hand" says Jesus. (Mark 1: 15)

As Christians, we hold the tension of blessing *and* sin in our lives and in our world. Glance at the nightly news, and we're reminded of the pervasiveness of sin. Humans commit unthinkable acts of violence. We put profits over people and the earth.

Though the media highlights these acts as what is most visible about humanity, what is invisible and hidden is our true nature of original blessing. We are made in the image and likeness of God.

Sin is all-encompassing in our society, but it does not define who we are. The Christian preoccupation with original sin has only exacerbated the dysfunction of our already violent society.

Don't get me wrong- we need to tell the truth, and not sugarcoat our foibles and failings. We need to take responsibility for the hurts we've caused. Yet our first task is to remind each other that we were born in blessing. Blessing and goodness is our true nature. Reframing our spiritual narrative means "detoxing our souls... from toxic religious teachings and ideologies. It calls for a great *unlearning.*"[18]

This will be the unlearning of beliefs that have no longer served us- beliefs that have kept us locked in ideas about who we are not, rather than who we are. This unlearning includes relearning the creation narrative as our primary narrative. It includes relearning the mystical strands of Jesus and Christianity that remind us of the sacredness of humanity and of all creation. Our relearning is a remembrance and awakening that we are called to be, live, and embody light and love in this world. Anything less is settling.

Augustine, in whom the original sin teaching originated, imagined that sin was inherent in human nature. Augustine spoke from his experience living sinfully for years, attached to his lower nature of sense pleasures, wealth, and worldly reputation. Despite Augustine's lofty aspirations, time and again he was unable to rise above his lower nature.

In a way, Augustine was not entirely wrong about sin. The truth is that we have everything inside us in the realm of consciousness- good,

18   Fox, Matthew, *Original Blessing*, (New York, Jeremy P. Tarcher/Putnam, 1983), 7-8.

bad, love, fear, altruism, lust, etc. Therefore we do well never to judge others. When we judge, it points out something unhealed which we judge most harshly in ourselves.

If everything is inside of us, then each of us has the potential for the highest good and the most horrific evils. The question is: which part of ourselves do we feed? If we feed the lower nature, it will grow stronger. If we do not feed our higher nature, day by day it will grow weaker, just as a muscle that atrophies over time.

Paramhansa Yogananda said, "thoughts are universally and not individually rooted."[19] Our task in feeding our higher nature is attunement. We attune ourselves with a consciousness that already exists (i.e., love, peace, joy). This takes persistence, patience, and practice. Too many people attune to their lower natures out of habitual default and peer pressure.

If we are surrounded by people who support us in our unhealthy habits, it will be increasingly difficult to change them. To quote Yogananda again, "Environment is stronger than will power."

Augustine is a perfect example of changing in the direction of our higher nature. Though it took Augustine many missteps and false starts, he finally made the leap to living a life for God alone. Augustine did this through determined willpower combined with the support of family and friends who were moving in the same spiritual direction (and all this by the grace of God).

If we are to tap into the original blessing that is our nature- pure love, unconditioned peace- we must be diligent in our spiritual habits, surround ourselves with uplifting spiritual community, and offer ourselves to grace, the real catalyst for change.

Saint Irenaeus said, "The glory of God is the glory of people fully alive." From Life we came, for Life we were created, and to Life we always return. The God of agape love created us by love, in love, and for love.

---

[19] Yogananda, Paramhansa, *Autobiography of a Yogi*, (Crystal Clarity Publishers, https://www.ananda.org/autobiography), Chapter 15.

We were created *as* a blessing, that we might *be* a blessing. Our task is to wake up, live fully alive, and spread Life (i.e., God) in all we do.

Each of us is as a wave on the ocean of Spirit. Though we are not the entirety of the ocean, the entirety of the ocean is contained in the wave. That which God is, we are. By our nature we are spiritual beings made in the image and likeness of God. This is our original blessing.

The same love that existed in Jesus also exists in us. Our potential, our calling, is to live into the same Christ-like love we see reflected in Jesus that also lives within our hearts. Amen.

CHAPTER SIX

THE BIBLE AND BELIEF

If many of us despair when we look at the world today, many also despair when we look at religion. Everywhere we turn, religion is used as a tool for violence.

At the time of writing this chapter, I recently returned from a trip to Israel and Palestine. Though inspired by sacred sites from the Christian and Jewish religions, I was also disheartened to see the violence that plagues this "holy" land- quite often a religiously motivated violence.

On September 11th, 2001, religiously motivated violence was felt in the United States as never before. In our grief, shock, and trying to make sense of what happened, most of us asked ourselves "How could someone, in the name of God, board a plane with the intention to kill others?!" Today, we continue to ask that question after tragedies like the suicide bombings and mass shootings that took the life of 130 people in Paris in November 2015.

Religious fundamentalism takes its most drastic form in suicide bombings, but its forms are present in every religion, including Christianity. Contrary to popular belief, the people who blow themselves up in the name of religion are normal people, like you and me. And normal people who trust religious "authorities" are often lured into false, potentially harmful beliefs.

The key to understanding fundamentalist behavior in any religion is one essential truth: **belief** *precedes* **action**. To my knowledge, ALL religiously based violence has come from beliefs or interpretations of sacred texts, traditions, or teachings.

Both terrorists **and** saints translate their beliefs into action, though it is rare to hear how the beliefs of saints manifest into action. Saint's mystical and often miraculous actions are little understood by the Western world and largely ignored by the media. Terrorists, who hold the flag of religion and utter the name of God while inflicting unspeakable violence, receive vast amounts of media coverage. The world's media overwhelmingly focuses attention on these stories, rather than the stories of saints, mystics, and sages whose religious beliefs translate into positive, beauty-filled actions.

In the Middle Ages, religiously motivated violence was perpetrated by Crusaders who pillaged whole cities of Jews and Muslims (and other ethnic and religious groups), carrying crosses before them, believing they carried out the will of God. What preceded these religious actions were beliefs- in this case, that recapturing "the Holy Land" of Jerusalem was God's will for the Christian faithful.

In the sacred texts of Islam, the word "jihad" has often been interpreted towards violent ends. Fundamentalists in Islam have blown up planes, buildings, and buses because of a belief that by performing these acts of violence they were fighting a "holy war."

Most Muslim adherents in the world call this belief a distortion of the true religion of Islam. On my trip to Israel and Palestine, one Muslim man shared with me, "The greatest misunderstanding of the Muslim faith today is that of jihad. People think it means holy war. All Muslims I know agree that 'jihad' was never intended to incite violence against innocent people." The Muslims that I know believe jihad means 'striving'- a lifelong effort to improve their character.

As Muslim fundamentalist beliefs are based on interpretations of the Koran, Christian fundamentalist beliefs are based on interpretations of the Bible.

The Bible is revered as sacred scripture in Christianity. Yet even to ask how many books are in the Bible leads to a difference in belief. While most Christians revere the same number of books in the New Testament, Catholics, Protestants, and Eastern Orthodox Christians count different numbers of books in the Old Testament, or Hebrew Bible.

What accounts for the difference? Belief.

Actions are based on beliefs, and our beliefs are filtered through how we interpret the world. How we interpret is rooted in the way we look at things- how we perceive. To change our actions, we must look to the core of consciousness- our perceptions.

For Jesus, the most effective way to transform undesirable behaviors was not to condemn the actions themselves, but to address the underlying beliefs. Whether it be about which foods to eat or how to keep the Sabbath, Jesus refrained from condemnation. Instead, he offered his audience a new perspective- sometimes through discourse, but often through parables. Jesus' stories engaged his listener's imagination, helping them look at life from another perspective.

Many people's negative experiences with the church have come from seeing judgmental, harmful Christian behaviors. Judgmental Christian behaviors have stemmed from judgmental beliefs. Unfortunately, many such beliefs have been sourced back to the Bible, or more accurately, to a literal interpretation of the Bible.

An "Evolutionary" Reading of the Bible

A Jewish colleague of mine recalls growing up in the 1950s and 60s in the United States, and being accosted by her Christian classmates: "Weren't you the ones who killed God?" For centuries, Christians believed Jews were the ones who killed Jesus Christ. This belief has justified violence against Jews as a sort of "eye for an eye."

These beliefs have not been isolated to the far past, but tragically were used to ignite violence in the Holocaust. In Germany, Christian beliefs were used as fuel to light the fire of Nazi hatred towards the Jewish people. Hitler and the Nazis perpetuated beliefs throughout Germany that Jewish people were subhuman- comparable to "parasites." The conclusion reached by Germans at that time had grave consequences: "What does the body do with parasites? It gets rid of them."

If belief is based on interpretation, and interpretation on perception, where did the perception come from that the Jews killed Jesus?

To answer this question, we must look deeply into how we interpret the Bible. Is the Bible's every word literally true? Does the Bible contain the "infallible" word of God that cannot be questioned or examined?

If the Bible does contain the infallible, unquestionable word of God, what are we to make of passages in the New Testament that go against modern ethical standards? Consider these two passages from the book of Ephesians:

"Wives, be subject to your husbands as you are to the Lord. For the husband is the head of the wife just as Christ is the head of the church, the body of which he is the Savior. Just as the church is subject to Christ, so also wives ought to be, in everything, to their husbands." (Ephesians 5: 22-24)

And:

"Slaves, obey your earthly masters with fear and trembling, in singleness of heart, as you obey Christ; not only while being watched, and in order to please them, but as slaves of Christ, doing the will of God from the heart." (Ephesians 6: 5-6)

If you have been turned off from the Bible, chances are it is from passages like these.

Nevertheless, to class the entire Bible as containing "Iron Age" interpretations of God and life is to throw the baby out with the bathwater. The Bible contains much eternal, timeless wisdom.

It is possible to interpret the Bible in such a way that honors its timeless truths, yet also honors the evolution of human life and thought (sometimes for good, sometimes not). Unfortunately, the old paradigm of scriptural interpretation- of infallibility and a "literal" interpretation of the Bible- does not generally afford such a view.

An infallible reading of scripture presents every Bible passage as the literal "Word of God." Translating such infallibility to the two Ephesians passages above, a literal reading says: wives, be subject to your husbands, and slaves, obey your masters (hence, condoning slavery).

Is this really the Christian teaching regarding women and slavery?

For those wounded by the church or turned off from judgmental beliefs rooted in scripture, there is an alternative interpretation. What if the Bible is both *inspired by* God and *people's experiences of* God? In that way, the Word of God in scripture is both human *and* divine, just like Jesus. The Bible is divinely inspired, but not without the filters of human experience.

Seen in this light, our danger is "making the Bible God, instead of seeing the Bible as writings that point to God."[20]

With this perspective, I read these two Ephesians passages as *people's experience of* God two thousand years ago, without feeling called to obey every word as literal truth for <u>my</u> life today.

This way of interpreting could be called an "evolutionary" reading of the Bible. It is another way of saying that as we evolve, scripture evolves.

The United Church of Christ puts it differently: "God is still speaking."

To say "God is still speaking" is to affirm the following: At one time, people heard God's voice in a particular way. In that context, God's "word" was a positive step for society. As society and people changed and evolved (or devolved), God spoke in different ways, according to differing needs and circumstances.

---

[20]   Flunder, Yvette: *Where the Edge Gathers: Building a Community of Radical Inclusion*, (Cleveland, The Pilgrim Press, 2005), p. 9.

In other words, God speaks to people <u>where they are</u>. God's words in one time and place aren't necessarily God's words in another setting. God's words to one people will not be God's words to another, different group of people.

Jesus himself modeled this in his teachings. In the Sermon on the Mount, Jesus repeats, "You have heard that it was said..., but I say to you..."

Jesus affirms that God spoke one way to the Jewish people thousands of years ago: "You have heard that it was said." (Matthew 5: 21) In the next breath, Jesus establishes that God hasn't stopped speaking: "but I say to you." (Matthew 5: 22)

As people evolve, God has a new word and a new message.

Later in the Sermon on the Mount, in Matthew 5: 38-39, Jesus says "You have heard that it was said, 'An eye for an eye and a tooth for a tooth.' But I say to you, do not resist an evildoer. But if anyone strikes you on the right cheek, turn the other also."

The original "eye for an eye" passage is found in Exodus Chapter 21 verses 22-25 of the Hebrew Bible. This "eye for an eye" teaching was a positive evolutionary step for society *at the time* of Exodus.

Before "eye for an eye," if someone took your eye, you might take their life. "Eye for an eye" meant a more equitable retribution- do not retaliate more, but in equal amount. If someone took your eye, you had the right to take their eye- nothing more.

Over a thousand years after "eye for an eye" was given as a commandment, Jesus knew that his Jewish listeners were ready to take this teaching to another level. In that spirit, he said "do not resist an evildoer." Don't take equal retribution for what they have taken from you.

In Jesus' day, this invitation was a positive evolutionary step.

Two notes of significance with this passage. First, Jesus' words illustrate the importance of understanding biblical context before assuming its "literal" meaning.

Contemporary society has commonly interpreted "turning the other cheek" as letting an evildoer stomp all over you. In other words, if a person slaps you, turn your cheek so they can slap you again. This interpretation takes Jesus' words far beyond their intended meaning.

In Jesus' day, there were subtle, underlying meanings to what it meant to slap someone. Slapping was done only with the right hand. The left hand, used for sanitary purposes, was seen as unclean and not used for slapping. Also, slapping with the *inside* of the right hand was an insult. It inferred that the other person was inferior to you. To slap with the *back* of the right hand, however, implied that the other person was equal to you- not inferior.

If someone slapped you using the inside of their right hand, they degraded you. If you turned your cheek, the perpetrator could only slap you with the back of their right hand. Thus, turning your cheek here is nonviolently asserting your equality.

In this context, "turning the other cheek" is a way of responding creatively to violence **without** violence.

Knowing a scripture's context- which we often don't- is critical to understanding its meaning. Bible passages read "literally," without a deeper understanding of context and motives, are not the whole picture.

A second important note is this: the church has historically used New Testament scriptures to claim that Jesus and Christianity are superior to Judaism and the Torah. Christian "supercessionism" is the term expressing this superiority, refering to Jesus' words "superseding" those of the Hebrew Bible, rendering them null and void.

Christians forget two important things in such a belief. First, Jesus lived and died as a faithful Jew. Second, Jesus never abolished the Jewish law, but kept it. Jesus says in the Sermon on the Mount, "Do not think that I have come to abolish the law or the prophets; I have come not to abolish but to fulfill." (Matthew 5: 17)

Jesus' message was not to abolish the law. He wanted people to remember the *spirit* of the law (love), not be legalistically attached to the *letter* of the law.

Jesus did not seek to abolish Judaism. He sought to increase the faithfulness, love, and compassion of Jews in his time.

Jesus knew that rules are helpful, but only to a point. When rules are worshipped as gods in themselves, we lose sight of the core message of love.

My Jewish friends today do not obey the Torah so strictly that "eye for an eye" is an authoritative teaching. Rabbinic teachings and millennia of "midrash" expound upon the Torah's meaning in greater depth. Rather than obey "eye for an eye," most rabbis I know teach their congregations to first obey the law of love, expressed by Rabbi Hillel nearly identically to Jesus: "What is hateful to you, do not to your fellow man. This is the law; all the rest is commentary." (Talmud, Shabbat 31a)

The idea that one religion is superior to another has caused untold violence to Jewish people and people of all races and religions over the course of millennia. Traditionally in the church, "salvation… hinges on the person of Christ… God's favor rests on those who recognize and participate in the saving work of Christ. The result is a sliding scale of humanity, by which persons of other faiths are seen as less than their Christian counterparts… when religion is bound up with culture, and where Whiteness has been bound up with Christianity, the supremacy of Christianity too easily slips into a supremacy of White Christianity."[21]

To be sure, Christianity, Judaism, and all religions have differences. Yet no religion or its scriptures are perfect. Each religion has saints, and each religion has adherents who have perpetrated violence in its name. Each religion has beautiful, poetic scriptures, and each has scriptures that make their adherents cringe.

In the Christian New Testament, passages about women and slavery are often a source of embarrassment for Christians. Christians

---

[21] Fletcher, Jeannine Hill, *The Sin of White Supremacy: Christianity, Racism, and Religious Diversity in America*, (New York, Orbis Books, 2017), 34, 36.

either shy away from reading such passages or dismiss them outright. But what if we looked at New Testament passages about women and slavery through an alternative, "evolutionary" lens?

Seen from an evolutionary perspective, these passages take on a new meaning. In the letter to the Ephesians, the woman is told to be subject to her husband. The husband, likewise, is exhorted to love his wife: "Husbands, love your wives, just as Christ loved the church and gave himself up for her... In the same way, husbands should love their wives as they do their own bodies. He who loves his wife loves himself." (Ephesians 5: 25-28)

At the time Ephesians was written in the first century, women were considered the property of men. Whether as wives or as daughters, women had few rights of their own, and were a great deal more dependent on men than today.

As a result, laws provided little safeguards for the health and safety of women. Husbands could more easily mistreat their wives (physically, verbally, or emotionally) without consequence.

Seen in that context, read this passage from Ephesians again: "Husbands, love your wives, just as Christ loved the church and gave himself up for her... husbands should love their wives as they do their own bodies. He who loves his wife loves himself."

The author of Ephesians tells husbands to love their wives- as they love their own bodies! The imagery is stark here. If you would not hurt or wish harm upon your own body, do not hurt or wish harm upon your wife.

While the author of Ephesians does not question the culturally acceptable practice of wives submitting to husbands, he does question the ill-treatment of wives by husbands.

The author doesn't go as far as we do today in advocating for women's rights but does make a positive evolutionary step.

The New Testament passage about slavery can be interpreted from the same evolutionary mindset. Living in contemporary times, we read the Ephesians text and think, "The Bible is saying slavery is okay. The Bible is even telling slaves to obey their masters!"

Slavery was common practice in those days, and not considered an ethical issue. For better or worse, few questioned this teaching. Given this reality in the first century, it isn't surprising that the author of this letter tells slaves to obey their masters.

When we read these words about slavery in their context, however, the author's words to slave masters here are blunt and direct: "And masters, do the same with them (the slaves). Stop threatening them, for you know that both of you have the same Master in heaven, and with him there is no partiality." (Ephesians 6: 9)

The author of Ephesians says something radical for the time: slaves are not lesser than their master and should not be mistreated. Before God, slave and master are equal. If the master shows unkindness to his slave, he will be held accountable for his behavior.

While this teaching was a positive moral step several thousand years ago, nevertheless we ask: "Why didn't the author go farther and condemn slavery altogether? Why didn't the author say that women and men were equal, and neither should be submissive or subservient to the other?"

Such questions are the tension we live with in an evolutionary reading, which upholds the eternal wisdom of the scriptures, while honestly grappling with the human bias and fallibility present throughout the Bible. Though inspired by God, the Bible does not always meet our contemporary ethical or social standards.

An evolutionary reading of scripture affirms that the Bible is inspired but not "perfect." Like us, the scriptures are colored by imperfect viewpoints and experiences.

Even when we claim to hear the voice of God- the inner voice of love- we do so through our own human filter. Even in the Bible, our most sacred Christian text, human and divine are intertwined in an intricate web of beauty, inspiration, and complication.

In an evolutionary reading of the Bible, head **and** heart are both essential to biblical interpretation. If we deconstruct texts with our head alone, the intellectual conclusions we reach will lack inspiration and integration. If we interpret with our heart divorced from reason (as many clergy encourage), too often we have "blind faith" without thinking critically about scriptures that don't resonate with our conscience and the inner voice of love.

Addressing Anti-Semitism from an "Evolutionary" Perspective

Jesus invited his disciples, imperfect though they were, to live from a place of love. Scriptures, like the humans that write them, are not perfect. Just as Jesus challenged people who were out of alignment with love, so Jesus challenged scriptures from the Hebrew Bible that didn't align with love.

In the centuries following Jesus' death, Jesus' followers wrote about his life, hoping to preserve his teachings, and the account of his life, for future generations. Four of these accounts (there were others) were included in the final Christian canon: Matthew, Mark, Luke, and John. Historically, many anti-Semitic readings of scripture are based out of the gospel of John.

The gospel of John is very different from the three synoptic gospels of Matthew, Mark, and Luke. John was written close to 100 C.E. (the last gospel chronologically), as "Christianity" was beginning to separate itself as something different and distinct from Judaism (Jesus and his first followers were all Jewish).

Many of the early followers of Jesus in the Johannine community were not welcome in other Jewish synagogues. Tension arose between these emerging Christians and the Jewish community. Some of that tension is evident throughout the gospel of John, where "the Jews" are referred to in derogatory terms. This tension isn't present in the earlier synoptic gospels.

The Gospel of John describes "the Jews" as the enemies of Jesus. In the gospels of Mark, Matthew, and Luke, the plot to kill Jesus is always seen coming from a small group of Jewish religious authorities, not from "the Jews" en masse.

Blaming the death of Jesus on "the Jews" is like blaming 9/11 on "the Muslims." This is just what was done after 9/11, resulting in much harm and prejudice inflicted on the Muslim community.

As John's gospel was being written, Jesus followers were being kicked out of temples. In the decades after Jesus was crucified, many early Christians were also crucified. These forms of mistreatment have a deep effect on the human psyche. Whenever a group of people experience trauma, such as the early Christians, or Americans post 9/11, our trauma has a lasting effect on our how we view the world, who is considered responsible for that violence, and how we move forward.

The writer/s of John's gospel were mired in conflict and tension, which is reflected in the gospel stories. From ancient until contemporary times, the Jewish people have been a convenient scapegoat.

As we discover the fallibility of the Bible, our temptation is to jettison it altogether.

Jesus modeled a radical re-interpretation of all scripture through the filter of love. This was Jesus' foundation, and it should be ours. Jesus invites us to ask the same questions that he asked: does scripture align with the God of unconditional, agape love? Do these stories and texts encourage all people to live from a place of expansive, inclusive love?

Given our historical penchant for misinterpreting sacred texts, questioning scripture is not a luxury. If we are to move in the direction of love, I dare say it is a necessity.

CHAPTER SEVEN

THE EGO IN RELIGION: SCIENCE AND SPIRITUALITY

A healthy, natural part of our maturity as a child is developing an ego- a separate, individual sense of "me," apart from others. As we grow older and mature, our task in the spiritual journey is to let go of our egos; to surrender our small, egoic "I" into the larger, infinite "I am." In the words of Eckhart Tolle, "The word 'I' embodies the greatest error and the deepest truth, depending on how it is used... In normal everyday usage, 'I' embodies the primordial error, a misperception of who you are, an illusory sense of identity. This is the ego."[22]

The nature of who we are is Oneness and interconnectedness. Gratifying the ego can be temporarily satisfying, but in the long term leads to emptiness and dissatisfaction. Happiness is found when we look not only to our needs, but the needs of others.

Spiritually, as we release the egoic "I," and mature into "the full stature of Christ" (Ephesians 4: 13), our sense of self becomes ever expansive. We see all other beings as the body of Christ- our own body- and so to be treated with the greatest care. The apostle

---

[22]   Tolle, Eckhart: *A New Earth: Awakening to Your Life's Purpose*, (New York, Penguin Group, 2005), 27.

Paul says, "as the body is one and has many members, and all the members of the body, though many, are one body, so it is with Christ… If one member suffers, all suffer together with it; if one member is honored, all rejoice together with it. Now you are the body of Christ and individually members of it." (1 Corinthians 12: 12, 26-27)

When we're locked in contractive consciousness, our lives are characterized by egoic reactions such as defensiveness. This is equally common in church settings as it is in secular ones. Going to church does not make anyone immune from egoic reactions. Churches are not perfect, just as people are not perfect. Both are perfectly imperfect!

Egoic reactivity lessens not from outer rituals, but from practicing new inner ways of being, and doing the difficult work of examining and transforming our defensive triggers from the inside, out.

No place does the ego have a tighter grip on humanity than our religious beliefs. This grip is difficult to loosen because for religious people, our beliefs are often our foundation! If our beliefs crumble, the entire religious foundation crumbles with it! Many have in this way experienced a crisis of faith.

As a result, churchgoers are skeptical and sometimes downright hostile towards insights from science or other spheres of learning that threaten their foundation.

On the contrary, science, being open to experimentation and new learnings, has progressed in many areas during the last four centuries. During this time, the church has regularly resisted new revelations from scientific exploration. Sensing that our foundation is in danger, Christians become defensive, fearing that who we are is under attack.

One of the first instances of this was with the physicist Galileo, who played a major role in the scientific revolution of the 17th century. Educated people in Galileo's time believed that the earth was the center of the universe, and all heavenly bodies revolved around the Earth. Galileo set forth a different idea, positing that the Earth and other planets revolved around a relatively stationary Sun at the center of the Solar System.

History tells us that Galileo was not only persecuted for his ideas but condemned by the Catholic Church for "vehement suspicion of heresy." The church judged Galileo's "error" through faulty, literal scriptural interpretations. For example, Psalm 104:5 states "the Lord set the earth on its foundations; it can never be moved." And Ecclesiastes 1:5 says, "And the sun rises and sets and returns to its place."

Egoic reactivity can manifest in any number of ways- including an incessant need to be right. From this lens, how insidious has the ego been in the life of the church- through the Crusades, the Spanish Inquisition, the Salem Witch trials, and many other instances!

Excessive attachment to being right has led to blanket church condemnations of scientific theories, and blanket scientific condemnations of religious beliefs, neither of which are helpful.

For example, does the account of God creating Adam and Eve mean that the creation of the world literally happened that way? Or could the Genesis creation narrative be a spiritual and metaphorical origin account, which offers deep meaning to our lives, but which doesn't (and wasn't meant to) tell the whole scientific picture?

With such a reading, we can welcome new scientific discoveries into our faith worldview. We can glean the spiritual wisdom from the account of creation in Genesis without leaving our mind at the door and neglecting prevailing scientific evidence about the Big Bang theory or evolution.

When scripture and science appear to contradict each other, we do well to ask: Is truth factuality alone? Or is truth something deeper than mere facts, pointing to a deeper spiritual reality? As we consider how to interpret scripture, there is much timeless wisdom in this Native American adage used to preface spiritual stories: "I don't know if it really happened this way, but I know this story is true."

When we release ourselves of the need for all scripture to be literally true, we loosen the grasp of the ego. This is of utmost importance in the church today when ego- in the name of virtue and religion- has committed countless atrocities. If we cannot release the grip of the ego in our lives and our faith communities, we will be slaves to our own ideas and judgments, whether those ideas are accurate or not.

Spiritual arrogance only leads to greater harm and destruction for people and for the planet. Our world now needs what Sir John Templeton once called 'humility theology', a "theology that acknowledges it does not have all the answers. We need a theology that is willing to continue asking questions."[23]

In his encounters with others, Jesus had infinite patience for people who struggled with questions and lost their way. Jesus' strongest words were reserved for scriptural literalists who taught religion as if they had all the answers, and worse, didn't live out their teachings! Here is but one example:

"Then Jesus said to the crowds and to his disciples, 'The scribes and the Pharisees sit on Moses' seat; therefore, do whatever they teach you and follow it; but do not do as they do, for they do not practice what they teach. They tie up heavy burdens, hard to bear, and lay them on the shoulders of others." (Matthew 23: 1-4)

Let us hold our beliefs and traditions lightly, remembering that our primary spiritual task is not proper doctrine, but the practice of love. We are called to ortho-praxis over and above ortho-doxy. Beliefs will arise out of our faith life, but correct doctrine isn't the kingdom of God. The kingdom of God is making God's love real on this earth, living out Jesus' prayer "Thy kingdom come, Thy will be done, on earth, as it is in heaven." May it be so.

---

[23] Walsch, Neale Donald, *The New Revelations: A Conversation with God*, (New York, Atria Books, 2002), 69.

CHAPTER EIGHT

HEAVEN, HELL, AND SALVATION

While beliefs are important in the spiritual life, they are no substitute for personal experience. So, when a church's doctrinal beliefs about God do not match with our personal experience of God, it is our responsibility to question ourselves *and* the church.

In this questioning, we measure our beliefs by the same metric Jesus did: love alone.

According to the belief system of many Christians, God created one right way home through Jesus Christ. Those who don't subscribe to this belief, who haven't "accepted Jesus as their Lord and Savior," are condemned to eternal damnation.

This belief has been so pervasive in Christian communities that "fire and brimstone" is part of everyday vernacular, referring to preachers who speak passionately about hell and God's punishment.

In this understanding, God's judgment of hell is reserved for those who don't believe the right thing, or those whose behaviors don't measure up to a particular Christian standard.

In our generation, Christian leaders claim that God's punishment is on those who don't live by heterosexual norms. Christian ministers such as Jerry Falwell have stated that AIDS is God's punishment for a homosexual lifestyle. When a man in Yvette Flunder's community was dying of AIDS, members of the dying man's family felt that

AIDS was God's final word of judgment on his "lifestyle" and punishment for his disobedience.[24]

Is this really the God of agape love that Jesus shared- the same God depicted in the parable of the prodigal son?

These beliefs "glorify Jesus at God's expense," forgetting the one Jesus came to reveal, portraying Jesus as Savior and God as "judge and executioner."[25] Such beliefs about God's punishment are a misalignment; a steering off course from the Way of Jesus.

Jesus does mention an afterlife in the gospels, but always in connection to how we treat persons in need. In Matthew 25: 31-46, our experience after life is directly proportional to how we treat the most vulnerable in this life - the hungry, the sick, the naked, the stranger, and the imprisoned. Jesus' story of the rich man and Lazarus points to discomfort in the afterlife ensuing from selfishness in this life (Luke 16: 19-31).

Scriptures that Christians cite referencing the afterlife are regularly taken out of context.

As the New Testament is a partial written record of the early Christians' spiritual journey, these scriptures contain much wisdom, but also mirror our humanity, not being free from the cultural lenses and biases of the time.

The scripture most often misinterpreted by Christians in reference to heaven and hell is John 14: 6: "I am the way, and the truth, and the life. No one comes to the Father except through me."

Many Christians understand this text to mean that anyone who doesn't believe in Jesus as Lord and Savior is condemned for eternity. Christians holding this worldview approach people of other faiths, or of no faith, through a lens of judgment and conversion.

Good and loving Christians will always disagree on how to interpret scripture. Nevertheless, let us remember how often

---

[24]   Flunder, Yvette: *Where the Edge Gathers: Building a Community of Radical Inclusion*, (Cleveland, The Pilgrim Press, 2005), p. 37.

[25]   Gulley P & Mulholland J., *If Grace is True: Why God Will Save Every Person*, (New York, HarperOne, 2003), 14.

Christian beliefs have been used to hurt, exclude, and judge others. There are two things to hold in mind so that we don't make the same mistakes.

The first is to prioritize love over belief, as Jesus did. In this way, we start relationships and conversations from a place of humility. Knowing that Jesus had strong words for those who clung too tightly to their religious beliefs and traditions, we do well not to claim that we hold THE universal truth or possess THE spiritual answers for eternity.

The second is to interpret scripture, traditions, and ideas as Jesus did- asking if they are rooted in love or in fear. When Jesus challenged the religious authorities in his day, he challenged their overly literal, harmful interpretations of the law. Might we, like the Pharisees and Sadducees before us, have unknowingly included exclusive, fearful elements in our beliefs?

Knowing that many harmful, exclusive Christian beliefs today are based on strict, literal interpretations of the Bible (as in Jesus' day), let us look at the text from John 14 more carefully.

When Jesus said, "I am the way, the truth, and the life," his Jewish disciples would have immediately recognized this reference. The "way," the "truth," and the "life" all refer to the Torah or the Law in Judaism. In this context, Jesus is saying that <u>he</u> is the way that his disciples are to follow, not strictly the Torah (Jesus also says in the gospel of Matthew 5: 17, "Do not think that I have come to abolish the law, I have come not to abolish but to fulfill.").

The context of the gospel of John here is important. As noted earlier, the writer/s of this gospel were in deep conflict with the established Jewish community. Many early Jesus followers in John's community were not welcome in Jewish synagogues. The tension between emerging Christians and the Jewish community is evident in the whole gospel of John, where "the Jews" are often referred to in a negative light.

Another important point is that Jesus' words in this text are pastoral in nature. In the verses before "I am the way..." Jesus says,

"You know the way to the place where I am going." (John 14: 4) In not so many words, Jesus is revealing to his disciples that he is soon leaving them. A distraught and confused Thomas replies, "Lord, we don't know where you are going, so how can we know the way?" (John 14: 5)

Jesus' response, "I am the way…" was a direct reply to Thomas' question. To distraught, grieving disciples, Jesus says that when they question what *way* to follow, remember that *the way is embodied in his life*. Jesus' pastoral statement is intended for his disciples then and now.

Jesus' words are not an exclusionary condemnation towards adherents of other religions. The "New Interpreter's Bible" says:

"It is a dangerous and destructive anachronism to cite John 14: 6-7 as the final arbiter in discussions of the relative merits of different religions' experiences and understandings of God. The fourth gospel is not concerned with the fate, for example, of Muslims, Hindus, or Buddhists, nor with the superiority or inferiority of Judaism and Christianity as they are configured in the modern world. These verses are the confessional celebration of a particular faith community, convinced of the truth and life it has received in the incarnation."[26]

John 14:6 is an affirmative statement, not an exclusionary one.

When I say to my wife LaToya: "You are the most beautiful woman in the world. No one is as beautiful as you," this is an affirmative statement. It is not meant to imply exclusivity and infer that other beautiful women don't exist.

Interpreting John 14:6 as an exclusionary statement takes Jesus' words out of context. These words are intended as an affirmative, confessional statement for an internal community.

Fire and brimstone interpretations of scripture are fear-based. They distort the God of love shown to us in the teachings, parables,

---

[26] Keck et al, eds., *New Interpreter's Bible*, (Abingdon Press, Nashville, 1995), 744-745.

and life of Jesus. In the gospels, Jesus tells parable after parable of a God who loves wandering prodigals and resentful sons; of a God who seeks after those who are lost ("lost" never being used in reference to people of other faiths). The God portrayed by Jesus is a God of extravagant, unconditional love. To interpret John 14:6 to say that God is an exclusive judge is unfair to the text and unfair to God.

Let us remember that our starting and ending point on the spiritual path is love. Love is Jesus' foundation, and he invites it to be ours as well.

If this is the case, then what are we to do with scriptures that seem to promote fear and judgment? Take "The fear of the Lord is the beginning of wisdom." (Psalm 111:10) or "Vengeance is mine, I will repay, says the Lord." (Romans 12:19)

Judgment and fear as the basis for Christian beliefs can be found throughout the Bible. Two thousand years ago, Jesus sought to move religious people away from beliefs rooted in fear and judgment. He knew that enough people were ready for the next step in their spiritual evolution. People were ready to live more deeply into the teachings of love and release beliefs constructed in fear and judgment.

As you can see, the church is a work in progress.

Beliefs based in love have the most solid biblical foundation of all. Jesus' greatest commandment was to "love the Lord your God with all your heart, and with all your soul, and with all your strength, and with all your mind; and your neighbor as yourself." (Luke 10: 27) Jesus repeatedly told the disciples "Be not afraid."

Fear and judgment have an important place on the evolutionary ladder. The fear of God as the beginning of wisdom has helped many otherwise nonreligious people contemplate divine realities. If "fear of the Lord" has helped thieves and murderers begin anew lives of service and compassion, then fear has indeed played a role as a positive evolutionary catalyst.

"Vengeance is mine, says the Lord" can be viewed as a positive spiritual step also. Instead of retaliating, this scripture verse has inspired many faithful Christians to reserve judgment for God. Unfortunately, this mentality has also led to harsh sentiments expressed by the same faithful churchgoers: "God will judge you for what you've done!"

Though fear and God's judgment can be positive steps directionally, the final step on our spiritual journey takes place when we release fear-based actions and beliefs and live out actions and beliefs solely from a place of love. The first letter of John says, "Perfect love casts out all fear. For those who fear have not been perfected in love." (1 John 4:18)

Jesus embodied this unconditional, expansive, perfect love. When a woman who had committed adultery came to Jesus followed by an angry mob, Jesus did not condemn her. With eyes of love and compassion, Jesus said to the crowd, "Let anyone among you who is without sin be the first to throw a stone at her." (John 8:7) One by one, the crowd dropped their stones and walked away.

"Judge not, and you will not be judged; condemn not, and you will not be condemned," (Luke 6:37) Jesus told his followers.

With that type of love, who wouldn't be drawn in deeper, wanting to learn and love more? This is the simple but not easy task of Jesus followers and communities today.

Try out this meditation for your spiritual practice today- as you breathe in, receive and open to the life-giving love that Jesus embodied and incarnated; as you breathe out, release any lingering beliefs in your consciousness rooted in fear. Breathe in love; breathe out fear. Repeat.

Some Christians say that our greatest task, even before love, is truth. Yet for Jesus, the greatest truth was love. The apostle Paul, who was touched and transformed by the unconditional love of Jesus, writes in his letters that when we speak our truth, we must do so in love (Ephesians 4:15). Another Pauline letter says, if I "understand all mysteries and knowledge... but don't have love, I am nothing." (1 Corinthians 13: 2)

Our priority in the Christian life is love, first and foremost. Truth is an expression of love, as it was for Jesus and the prophets before him. If our truth is out of alignment with agape love, we must question its source.

The "truth" that has most consistently turned Christians and non-Christians away from the church has been traditional Christian teachings about heaven and hell.

"Fire and brimstone" aren't the core message of Christianity or Jesus. Love is.

Now certainly, when our lives aren't in alignment with the law of love, there will be consequences. This is where the wisdom of "hell" can be found- not in a God who condemns sinners, atheists, or non-Christians, but in the personal and societal hells which individuals and society co-creates in the here and now.

Many Christian theologies that teach hellfire and damnation do affirm that God is love. As the reasoning goes, however, God granted us free will. With that free will, if we decide to live an unacceptable lifestyle, or don't subscribe to the right belief system, God's hands are tied. God *would* love to send us to heaven but *has to* send us to hell. Our deeds or beliefs deserve it.

The inconsistency of this view is obvious. Yes, God has given us free will, so will not interfere with our poor choices. But to declare God must send us to perish in eternal damnation makes God into an oppressive, abusive parent. What loving parent would send their child to time out forever? Don't loving parents want their children to learn and grow from their mistakes? Doesn't God want the same for us?

God's hands are not tied. God created a system of consequence, not of rewards and punishments. "You reap whatever you sow" says the apostle Paul in Galatians 6: 7. Consequence is the natural outcome of our actions, built into the system of life. If I put my hand into the fire for too long, it will get burned. That isn't God's punishment.

God desires all of us to live a life of fullness and joy. "I have said these things to you so that my joy may be in you, and that your joy may be complete." (John 15: 11) Jesus says.

And again, "I came that they may have life, and have it abundantly" (John 10:10)

God's love for us is eternal, unconditional, and unwavering. God is the devoted father who waits for the prodigal to come home. God is the caring mother who more than anything wants her children to lead happy, fulfilling lives. When we lose our way, God is the shepherd who searches sleeplessly for the one lost sheep (Luke 15: 3-7), or the woman who searches all over for her one lost coin:

"Or what woman having ten silver coins, if she loses one of them, does not light a lamp, sweep the house, and search carefully until she finds it? When she has found it, she calls together her friends and neighbors, saying, 'Rejoice with me, for I have found the coin that I had lost.' Just so, I tell you, there is joy in the presence of the angels of God over one sinner who repents." (Luke 15: 8-10)

Beliefs engrained in condemnation and judgment don't accurately portray the God of agape love who always wants our highest and best. Each of us is precious to God. God loves us, and there is NOTHING we can do about it!

CHAPTER NINE

HOMOSEXUALITY: WHAT JESUS SAID

Jesus had this to say about homosexuality:

Nothing! Jesus said nothing about homosexuality.

Churches over the centuries have followed suit, often saying nothing, or more frequently, condemning same-sex behaviors as sinful. Many churches today subscribe to "don't ask, don't tell" and "hate the sin, love the sinner" approaches.

My journey connecting spirituality and same-sex relationships started in confusion. I grew up in high school and college in a progressive household and an inclusive church. Since I identify as a heterosexual, cisgender male attracted to cisgender females, I didn't think much about how faith connected to homosexuality, let alone the spectrum of LGBTQIA (Lesbian, Gay, Bisexual, Transgender, Queer & Questioning, Intersexual, Asexual).

When I went to Belize as a Jesuit Volunteer after college, I met Christians who were confident in their faith-based approach condemning homosexual behaviors. This confidence, they told me, was rooted in biblical beliefs. Since I was not as biblically literate, I felt at a loss for how to respond to these scriptural conjectures.

Growing up surrounded mostly by other heterosexual males and females, gay, lesbian, bisexual, or transgender persons rarely crossed paths with me (to my knowledge). Heterosexual relations between a male and a female seemed normative- certainly for me, but also for most of my peers.

Were heterosexual relations not simply normative, but God's will and intention for humanity? Through education, I began to see that the lack of visibility of LGBTQIA persons was not because they didn't exist, but because of the great judgment towards those who "came out." Blinded by my own privilege, I had been unaware how much courage it took to come out in the face of what was sure to be condemnation and violence from strangers and even from loved ones.

If LGBTQIA persons were willing to risk so much simply to affirm who they were, was being gay really a choice? I reflected on my own sexual attraction to females. I had never made a conscious choice about which gender I was attracted to. It simply felt natural, like an organic part of me. If the same was true for those attracted to the same gender, who was I to judge or condemn? The words of Jesus rang clearly in my mind: 'Do not judge, and you will not be judged; do not condemn, and you will not be condemned.' (Luke 6: 37)

In the face of Jesus' silence on this issue, who were Christians to boldly proclaim God's judgment on same-sex relations?

After time and reflection, I finally felt confident in affirming that consensual same-sex relationships were not a sin, but a blessing. Reason and experience had helped me to reach this conclusion.

In Christianity, the authorities of reason and experience often do not factor as heavily as scripture and church tradition. In my conversations with Christians who were confident in their judgments, reason and experience seemed to take a back seat to the authority of scripture.

When I began seminary in 2004, I was eager to dig deeper into God's will with respect to same-sex marriage. My primary reflection question was not simply "What would Jesus do?" Many contemporary moral questions Jesus didn't specifically address in his day. If God is still speaking, then what was Jesus' message today relating to this question?

And if I am not separate from God or Jesus, then the deepest answers were beyond my ego, at the level of the soul. Accordingly, I sought to quiet my ego and preconceived ideas so that I could listen to God's still-speaking voice within.

One clear insight from my listening and study is that scripture is not a black and white book of rules to be followed unquestioningly for all time. The Bible is a collection of stories about God and God's people. As presented in Chapter 5, the morals found in the Bible are evolutionary, and must be understood in the context of each scripture.

I will not explore every Bible passage that has been referenced with regards to homosexuality in this book. Other sources listed in the footnotes have already done that more thoroughly than I.

Christian beliefs about the sinfulness of homosexuality claim to be rooted in scripture. And yet, most of the scriptures that refer to same-sex relations do not refer to homosexuality.

In the context of the Old Testament, for example, references connecting Sodom and Gomorrah to homosexuality are inaccurate. Homosexuality refers to relationships of mutual consent between persons of the same gender. The sin of the Sodomites was homosexual *rape* carried out by heterosexuals intent on humiliating strangers by treating them "like women," thus demasculinizing them. This brutal gang-rape has nothing to do with the problem of whether genuine love expressed between consenting persons of the same sex is legitimate or not.

Two of the three texts in the Bible that many Christians use to condemn homosexuality are from the book of Leviticus. Leviticus 18:22 states: "You shall not lie with a male as with a woman; it is an abomination." Leviticus 20:13 adds a penalty to this act: "If a man lies with a male as with a woman, both of them have committed an abomination; they shall be put to death, their blood is upon them."

The laws in the Torah applied to a particular people at a particular time. Not all the laws in Leviticus, Numbers, and Deuteronomy were universal. We don't see Christians shouting from the pulpits in church, "Don't sit where a menstruating woman sat" (Leviticus 15:19-21), or "A woman suspected of adultery must drink dirty water" (Numbers 5:11-31), or "Don't plant more than one kind of seed in a field." (Leviticus 19:19)

When we read these passages, we know that these laws were contextual to the Israelites thousands of years ago. We don't universalize them to our society today. Yet, we have selectively chosen some of these rules that fit our predetermined worldview.

The reason that homosexual acts were considered "an abomination" at the time of the Hebrew Bible is that the common Jewish understanding was that semen contained the whole of emerging life. As a result, "the spilling of semen for *any* nonprocreative purpose -- in coitus interruptus (Gen. 38:1-11), male homosexual acts or male masturbation -- was considered tantamount to abortion or murder."[27] That this text refers to the "sin" of spilling semen is further illustrated by the observation that female-to-female sexual activity is not prohibited in the Torah. The prohibition of male-to-male sexual acts also reflects the patriarchal culture of that time:

"When a man acted like a woman sexually, male dignity was compromised. It was a *degradation,* not only in regard to himself, but for every other male. The patriarchalism of Hebrew culture shows its hand in the very formulation of the commandment, since no similar stricture was formulated to forbid homosexual acts between females."[28]

Leviticus states that two males committing sexual acts together must be executed. The Torah also commands that people be put to death for striking their parents, cursing their parents, or being a stubborn or rebellious son (to name a few). Do any Christians take these scriptural texts literally today?

The Hebrew scriptures do not have clear examples of what we know of today as *homosexuality*- i.e., relationships of mutual consent between persons of the same gender. All same-sex behavior in the "Old Testament" contains violent and exploitative sexual expressions: "Genesis 19 and Judges 19 both identified male-male sexual activity with violent gang rape. Surveying the entire Old Testament, I could find only one other unambiguous description of males lying with males: This involved male cult prostitutes... found in Deuteronomy 23:17, 1 Kings 14: 24; 15:12, 22:46, and 2 Kings 23:7."[29]

How do we know if a sexual behavior aligns with love and mutual consent or not? Rather than take soundbites from the Bible

[27] Wink, Walter, *Biblical Perspectives on Homosexuality,* http://www.religion-online.org/showarticle.asp?title=1265

[28] Wink, Walter, *Biblical Perspectives on Homosexuality,* http://www.religion-online.org/showarticle.asp?title=1265

[29] Achtemeier, Mark, *The Bible's YES to Same-Sex Marriage: An Evangelical's Change of Heart,* (Louisville, Westminster John Knox Press, 2014), 82.

to support black and white answers, let's instead acknowledge that sexual morality is shades of grey (a little pun intended).

As we delve into the morality of any relationship or behavior, it is best to inquire about context rather than make universal assumptions. I personally like the three-fold questions offered by my seminary professor Leanne Tigert: What is the meaning? What is the motive? What is the consequence?

The Hebrew scriptures condemn the only known same-gender sexual behaviors at the time: rape and prostitution. Contemporary society does not ethically approve of those behaviors either. Exploitation and power, not love and mutual consent, are the motives behind such behaviors. Violence, abuse, and trauma are most often the consequence.

The biblical writers who taught against same-sex behaviors weren't referring to homosexuality as we know it in contemporary society. Indeed, these ancient writers knew "nothing that remotely resembles the loving, egalitarian, committed gay marriages and partnerships that we know today."[30]

The third biblical text most often referenced in condemning homosexual behavior comes from Romans 1: 26-27:

"For this reason God gave them up to dishonorable passions. Their women exchanged natural relations for unnatural, and the men likewise gave up natural relations with women and were consumed with passion for one another, men committing shameless acts with men and receiving in their own persons the due penalty for their error."

The community in Rome, including Paul (the author of the letter to the Romans), weren't familiar with what we know of today as "sexual orientation." Sexual orientation is an individual quality that inclines people to romantic or sexual attraction to the opposite sex or gender, to the same sex or gender, or to both sexes or more

---

[30] Achtemeier, Mark, *The Bible's YES to Same-Sex Marriage: An Evangelical's Change of Heart*, (Louisville, Westminster John Knox Press, 2014), 82.

than one gender (or, in the case of those identified as asexual, to none of the above).

Paul, being unfamiliar with sexual orientation, is referring to sexual behavior, over which we have a high degree of choice. It is Paul's assumption "that those whom he condemns are heterosexual, and are acting contrary to nature, "leaving," "giving up," or "exchanging" their regular sexual orientation for that which is foreign to them. Paul knew nothing of the modern psychosexual understanding of homosexuals as persons whose orientation is fixed early in life, persons for whom having heterosexual relations would be acting contrary to nature, "leaving," "giving up" or "exchanging" their usual sexual orientation."[31]

Additionally, Paul uses the word "natural" differently than we think of "natural" today. In the context of the Christian scriptures, "Paul uses 'natural' not in a biological or anatomical sense, but as a description of behaviors that are in line with prevailing customs and expectations. For example, Paul uses the same Greek word to suggest that 'nature' teaches it is degrading for men to wear their hair long (1 Cor. 11: 14)."[32] If it's unnatural for men to wear their long hair, then I lived "unnaturally" for over 10 years after college!

Paul is referring to relationships dominated by lust and abuse. He is not describing relationships characterized by long-term commitment and love. Paul, like the biblical writers of the Hebrew scriptures before him, had no understanding of sexual orientation and no examples in the Greco-Roman culture of same-sex relationships based on mutual consent and care.

The only known same-sex behaviors found in New Testament times were violent or exploitative: military victors who raped prisoners of war; masters who took advantage of slaves as a demonstration of dominance; homosexual prostitution practiced as part of pagan

---

[31] Wink, Walter, *Biblical Perspectives on Homosexuality*, http://www.religion-online.org/showarticle.asp?title=1265

[32] Achtemeier, Mark, *The Bible's YES to Same-Sex Marriage: An Evangelical's Change of Heart*, (Louisville, Westminster John Knox Press, 2014), 96.

worship; and pederasty- a social arrangement where young boys provided sexual favors to older men in exchange for philosophical training and social patronage.[33]

In Paul's theology, "venereal disease is the divine punishment for homosexual behavior" whereas today, "we know it as a risk involved in promiscuity of every stripe, but would hesitate to label it a divine punishment."[34]

In Paul's worldview, homosexuality is contrary to nature. Today, we know that homosexuality is "manifested by a wide variety of species, especially (but not solely) under the pressure of overpopulation. It would appear then to be a quite natural mechanism for preserving species."[35]

No Christian reads every word of the Bible literally. To do so would mean favoring the death penalty for unlawful religious infractions or disobedience towards one's parents. Is this really the message of compassion, forgiveness, and love that Jesus came to share?

Jesus asks us to read scripture through the lens of love. Love is the essence of any religious law. Literal interpretations too often confuse form with essence.

Ideally, the form of any law is an outward expression of the inner spirit of love. The outer form of a behavior is not what is most important, because forms always change. What is most important is the inner essence of any form, rule, law, or behavior.

There are many sexual behaviors found in scripture whose morality, based solely on biblical texts, is ambivalent. For example, "most of us would regard as taboo intercourse with animals, incest, rape, adultery, prostitution, polygamy, levirate marriage and

---

[33]   Achtemeier, Mark, *The Bible's YES to Same-Sex Marriage: An Evangelical's Change of Heart*, (Louisville, Westminster John Knox Press, 2014), 92-93.

[34]   Wink, Walter, *Biblical Perspectives on Homosexuality*, http://www.religion-online.org/showarticle.asp?title=1265

[35]   Wink, Walter, *Biblical Perspectives on Homosexuality*, http://www.religion-online.org/showarticle.asp?title=1265

concubinage -- even though the Old Testament permits the last four and the New Testament is silent regarding most of them."[36]

If the Bible is unclear, how are we to make decisions about which of these acts is ethical and which is not?

The Bible is a collection of different writings from a wide range of authors. Compiled by early Hebrew religious authorities (the Old Testament) and early Christian religious authorities (the New Testament), the Bible is not one genre, but many. These genres include story, poetry, prophecy, law, teachings, parables, letters, revelation, and more.

As a wide mix of collections, written by an even wider array of persons, the Bible has no one clear teaching on any number of ethical concerns. There are plenty of sexual attitudes and practices common in the Bible that we reject today, including "biblical attitudes and practices regarding nudity, intercourse during menstruation, prudery about speaking of the sexual organs and act, the "uncleanness" of semen and menstrual blood, endogamy, levirate marriage, and social regulations based on the assumption that women are sexual properties subject to men."[37]

If our decisions regarding these sexual matters are not biblically based, then what is our foundation for decision-making? Walter Wink asserts that the Bible does not have a sex ethic, but only a "love ethic." It is this love ethic that we constantly bring to bear on whatever sexual mores are dominant in any given country, culture, or period."[38] Jesus does not give us easy answers to every question about sexual morality. The Bible is not a quick "Complete Idiot's Guide" answer book for every contemporary ethical inquiry.

---

[36] Wink, Walter, *Biblical Perspectives on Homosexuality*, http://www.religion-online.org/showarticle.asp?title=1265

[37] Wink, Walter, *Biblical Perspectives on Homosexuality*, http://www.religion-online.org/showarticle.asp?title=1265

[38] Wink, Walter, *Biblical Perspectives on Homosexuality*, http://www.religion-online.org/showarticle.asp?title=1265

In the gospel of Luke, Jesus says, "Why do you not judge for yourselves what is right?" (Luke 12:57) In many Christian and religious circles, we would rather be told what to do than think critically and judge for ourselves. This attitude is manifest as unquestioning obedience to religious authorities and church tradition.

Ironically, in the Bible Jesus questions religious authorities and tradition more than anyone!

In Jesus' day, as in ours, it is common for religious leaders to lose sight of the ultimate goal of love. To the extent that we lose sight of love while interpreting scripture or tradition, Jesus invites us to repent and be transformed.

Jesus' own words convey the radical freedom that God gives us, and that we are invited to exercise in our lives and decision-making. "Judge for yourselves" says Jesus in Luke 12: 57. In other words, do not blindly accept the teachings of others who are in authority. Look to your own inner wisdom. Paul himself says, "Do you not know that we are to judge angels? How much more, matters pertaining to this life!" (1 Cor. 6:3).

Paul did not expect that his letters would become new laws for living. In the words of Wink, "The last thing Paul would want is for people to respond to his ethical advice as a new law engraved on tablets of stone. He is himself trying to "judge for himself what is right." If now new evidence is in on the phenomenon of homosexuality, are we not obligated -- no, *free* -- to re-evaluate the whole issue in the light of all available data and decide, under God, for ourselves? Is this not the radical freedom for obedience which the gospel establishes?"[39]

---

[39]   Wink, Walter, *Biblical Perspectives on Homosexuality*, http://www. religion-online.org/showarticle.asp?title=1265

CHAPTER TEN

PLURALISM: BEING CHRISTIAN IN A WORLD OF MANY FAITHS

As a Christian clergy, I'm sometimes asked why I do interfaith work. What is the point? What does it mean to be Christian in a society that is religiously pluralistic? How do interfaith experiences contribute to my own identity as a Christian?

With so much religiously motivated violence, war, discrimination, and fear in our world, my first thought is usually- how can I *not* do interfaith work? In such circumstances, how can I not work for greater peace and unity among religions?

We do not live in a homogenous religious environment, as previous generations did. People of other faiths are our neighbors, students, and friends; they are the people across town and the people next door. Asking questions about the meaning of interfaith is not a luxury. It's a necessity.

For ten years up until 2014, I was the Program Director of Interfaith Youth Initiative (IFYI), a week-long gathering of high school and college youth from Jewish, Christian, Muslim, Hindu, Buddhist, Humanist, and other spiritual backgrounds. This gathering of youth and staff mentors from across religions modeled for me the possibility of what interfaith relations could look like in our world today.

One of the first and most powerful things we did at IFYI was to create collective agreements together. These included "non-negotiables" like no drugs or sex during our program. After those were clear, we always asked, "What do we need to create a peaceful, harmonious, safe space for these eight days?"

The agreements that the high school and college youth came up with during IFYI were always remarkable. Even more remarkable was the way the IFYI youth lived these agreements out. Regularly during the week, community "check-ins" gave the youth a chance to share how the community was doing at living out the agreements they had co-created. What are our strengths and our growing edges? What can we celebrate, and what do we need to work on?

This creating of a safe container is the most important part in any interfaith gathering. To open up, people must know that they can be free to be who they are- in a religious sense, but also with other aspects of their identity.

In this safe and brave space, deep, honest communication flowed easily. Knowing they were safe to be who they were, barriers come down. Even as trust deepened during the IFYI program, conflicts inevitably arose. The collective agreements and safe container were the foundation that allowed this community to come out of those conflicts stronger and more mature.

Conflicts at IFYI sometimes fell into the personality category, and other times into the religious category. Personality conflicts are a natural part of our human condition. Through small group settings, one-on-one conversations, and workshops on peacemaking skills (such as active listening, nonviolence, and mediation), we trained the IFYI youth to be peacemakers in their communities and in their individual lives.

Religious conflicts, on the other hand, are often in the realm of misperceptions, judgments, or stereotypes. In a world generally skeptical of religion, many stereotypes exist of people from all religious backgrounds. Conflict resolution includes religious education. "No, not all Muslims believe that jihad means holy war through violence."

Stereotypes and judgments are best dealt with through heartfelt, honest communication and relationship building. "I have a great new Muslim friend. It's really been powerful for me. Before that, I had only heard about Muslims in connection with terrorist events."

Tolerance can be a good first step in interfaith settings when you contrast it to the alternative. However, tolerance is a limiting word. How many of us hope to be "tolerated" by others? Beyond tolerance, the goal of IFYI is to deeply understand each other, realizing the deep interconnectedness inherent in life and in the human family.

We learn about the "other," not only to understand them, and not only to have compassion for them, but to realize that we are not separate from them. Their struggles are our struggles; their pain, our pain; their joy, our joy.

In the end, education about the "other" causes us to realize that there is no "other." There is no "us" versus "them." There is only "we." We are all in this together and we are all one- a truth expressed in most major world religions.

Other times in religious conflict, deep-seeded beliefs need to be addressed. Say, for example, a belief that one religion is superior to others- their way is the "right" way; other ways are simply wrong.

Relationship building is usually sufficient to plant seeds of doubt concerning our judgments of others. "I met this great new humanist friend. I have trouble believing that God would condemn her just because she doesn't belong to my religion or subscribe to my beliefs."

In all cases, humanizing the "other" is the best way of countering ideas of religious superiority ("I am better than you"), condemnation ("you're going to hell if you don't believe what I believe"), or conversion ("you need to become exactly like me").

Not all religious conflicts will be resolved in safe, brave interfaith spaces like IFYI. Some deeply ingrained beliefs will not budge, particularly when we are hoping for another to change. That is part of interfaith engagement too.

Many of us who are religiously progressive (myself included), have an intolerance for intolerance. But the heart of interfaith engagement is developing understanding and compassion for those who are difficult to love, including those we label "intolerant."

In creating a safe space where all views, opinions, and beliefs can be shared openly and honestly, we must be willing at times to agree to disagree- to honor the belief of another, even when their belief doesn't resonate with our own truth.

Creating a safe interfaith space is an experiment in building and living beloved community together. In more than 10 years of building beloved communities at IFYI, the result was always far greater than I anticipated or imagined. About IFYI, we always told visitors and inquirers: "You have to see it to experience it for yourself."

While intentionally creating beloved community, something deep happens in the group formation process. A safe interfaith space becomes a place where my faith is enriched by your faith.

It's hard to say when this happens, but when it does, it pervades the entire community. We may challenge one another, but in the end, we grow because of our interactions. I am a better Christian because of my interactions with the Jews, Muslims, Humanists, Hindus, Buddhists, and others who have been part of the IFYI community over the years. Through workshops, interfaith "circles," days of interfaith dialogue, service, and small group sharing, I have been deeply inspired by persons representing faith traditions other than my own.

Interfaith is not a "watering down" of anybody's faith, or a place for evangelization or conversion. Interfaith, at its best, is a place where we learn deeply from our friends of other traditions, getting to know the real them. As we drop our stereotypes and preconceptions, we move into a place of mutual enrichment. In this place, sometimes we are challenged by, and other times inspired by, the faith traditions of others. In the end, we come away with a deep appreciation for the religious plurality and diversity in our world, as expressed in this poem by the Dalai Lama:

Religious Diversity

All religions share a common root, which is limitless compassion.
They emphasize human improvement, love, respect for others, and compassion for the suffering of others.
In so far as love is essential in every religion, we could say that love is a universal religion.
But the various techniques and methods for developing love differ widely between the traditions.
I don't think there could ever be just one single philosophy or one single religion.
Since there are so many different types of people, with a range of tendencies and inclinations, it is quite fitting that there are differences between religions.
And the fact that there are so many different descriptions of the religious path shows how rich religion is.
- His Holiness the XIV Dalai Lama

Giving Christianity back to agape love (for me) involves embracing religious pluralism. Diana Eck of "The Pluralism Project" classifies pluralism through four points:

"First, pluralism is not diversity alone, but the energetic engagement with diversity. Second, pluralism is not just tolerance, but the active seeking of understanding across lines of difference. Third, pluralism is not relativism, but the encounter of commitments. The new paradigm of pluralism does not require us to leave our identities and our commitments behind, for pluralism is the encounter of commitments. It means holding our deepest differences, even our religious differences, not in isolation, but in relationship to one another. Fourth, pluralism is based on dialogue. Dialogue means both speaking and listening, and that process reveals both common understandings and real differences."[40]

Pluralism is the first step in healthy interfaith relationships. Giving Christianity back to agape love goes a step beyond pluralism. In this step, we not only dialogue and embrace differences. We welcome the wisdom and beauty found in all traditions rooted in love, recognizing that saints of all religions offer spiritual nuggets and practices that deepen our unique religious identity.

Some Christians adamantly assert that all practices and wisdom learned in churches must come from Christian scriptures or Christian tradition. Yet Jesus himself was not so closed-minded:

"John answered, 'Master, we saw someone casting out demons in your name, and we tried to stop him, because he does not follow with us.' But Jesus said to him, 'Do not stop him; for whoever is not against you is for you.'" (Luke 9: 49-50)

Too often we, like the disciples, try to put Jesus and Christianity in a box. But Jesus and God don't fit neatly into boxes. Jesus' wildly universal love and God's abundant grace will always be set free from whatever restrictions we put on it.

There are Christians today (myself included) who practice yoga, go to retreats devoted to mindfulness, offer the healing energy of reiki, and attend kirtans chanting songs in Sanskrit. Is this wrong? Would Jesus disapprove? Or would Jesus respond today as to the disciples of old: "Whoever is not *against* you is *for* you."

Embodied practices such as yoga, mindfulness, or kirtan chanting offer a level of spirituality and devotion that many Christians see in Jesus but haven't found in the church. Christians and non-Christians alike hunger for the depth they see in Jesus, but that has been absent in churches.

God is beyond any one religion. Spirit doesn't care whether you say a prayer to "Allah", "Jehovah", or "Father." The Divine Mother

---

[40]   Eck, Diana, *What is Pluralism*, http://pluralism.org/pluralism/what_is_pluralism

doesn't care whether you chant to Her in English or Sanskrit. What is most important to God is the heart. "The Lord does not see as mortals see; they look on the outward appearance, but the Lord looks on the heart." (1 Samuel 16: 7) Jesus himself says, "There is nothing outside a person that by going in can defile, but the things that come out are what defile." (Mark 7:16)

Spiritual practices like yoga, mindfulness, reiki, and kirtan have made me a better Christian.

Christianity has its share of contemplative, embodied practices. Overall, however, Christianity is just catching on that many people are leaving church because they don't find spiritual depth or abundant life within it. Many people find more life in retreat centers, yoga classes, and hikes than they do in church. Christian faith communities, with some exceptions, have not offered embodied, devotional practices that help people deepen their spiritual lives and fill their spiritual cups. Is it any surprise that many Christians have turned to Hinduism, Buddhism, or to mystical traditions such as Sufism? "Recovering" Christians see the rigidity of the institutional church as another way that church has become like the Pharisees-putting dogma and doctrine above love and spiritual growth.

The first thing Jesus says in the gospel of Mark is "repent, and believe in the good news." (Mark 1: 15) I pray that we Christians repent of our spiritual rigidity and live into the openness and depth that we see clearly in Jesus.

God is in all religions, not just Christianity. To live into this knowing is to honor the many practices and paths by which people find God and fill their spiritual cups.

Our world is crying out for something like this, something that Roman Catholic Brother Wayne Teasdale called "Interspirituality":

"The real religion of humankind can be said to be spirituality itself, because mystical spirituality is the origin of all of the world's religions. If this is so, and we believe it is, we might also say that interspirituality -- the sharing of ultimate experiences across traditions-- is the religion of the third millennium. Interspirituality is the foundation that can prepare the way for a planet-wide-enlightened culture, and a continuing community among the religions that is substantial, vital, and creative."[41]

"Interspirituality" is not a watering down of Christianity, or a turning away from the message of Jesus. It is a recognition that God can work in and through anyone and can fill our cups with grace in the least expected of ways.

Religion and spirituality are about tapping into what gives us life and sharing that with others. Spirituality "is always about what nourishes. Tradition is useful as long as it enhances and serves the inner life. When it becomes an obstacle, we need to rethink the hold our religion has on us."[42]

Brother David Steindl-Rast is a Benedictine monk who puts interfaith and interspiritual encounters in these terms: there is a "distinction between being *rooted* in your tradition and being stuck in it. The point is to have roots that nourish, rather than a desperate clinging that chokes off real spiritual vitality."[43]

I was blessed with open-minded parents and grandparents, who exposed me to spiritual teachings within and outside of my Christian tradition during and after college. Two of the spiritual teachers I was exposed to at that time, Paramhansa Yogananda and Thich Nhat Hanh, resonated deeply with me. Their teachings in yoga, meditation, and mindfulness stay with me to this day. Though I do not identify as Hindu or Buddhist, my spiritual journey has benefitted immensely by learning from these enlightened Hindu and Buddhist masters. Paramhansa Yogananda and Thich Nhat Hanh

---

[41] Teasdale, Wayne, *The Mystic Heart: Discovering a Universal Spirituality in the World's Religions*, (Novato, CA, New World Library, 2001), 26.

[42] Teasdale, Wayne, *The Mystic Heart: Discovering a Universal Spirituality in the World's Religions*, (Novato, CA, New World Library, 2001), 20.

[43] Teasdale, Wayne, *The Mystic Heart: Discovering a Universal Spirituality in the World's Religions*, (Novato, CA, New World Library, 2001), 20.

provided me much needed spiritual food that had been missing in my Christian circles.

Benedictine monk John Main was one catalyst who inspired Christian meditation in the last century. Main's encounter with meditation through Swami Satyananda in Malaysia in the 1950s was the catalyst for the resurgence Christian meditation in recent times. Main's encounter with a Hindu guru didn't make him less Christian. On the contrary, it deepened his Christian roots.

Our encounter with other spiritual traditions has the potential to be not only informative, but transformative. Rather than being a doctrinal "no-no," such crossing-over has given spiritual life and vitality to many persons who remain firmly rooted within their own tradition. Interspiritual sharing is not a threat to our tradition. Instead, we can welcome the spiritual riches we gain from these encounters. In the words of Brother Teasdale, "We don't reject our own tradition, but build on it."[44]

---

[44]   Teasdale, Wayne, *The Mystic Heart: Discovering a Universal Spirituality in the World's Religions*, (Novato, CA, New World Library, 2001), 49.

CHAPTER ELEVEN

JESUS & GOD

It is a curious thing what we Christians have done with Jesus. All throughout the gospels, Jesus points not to himself, but to God. "Why do you call me good," Jesus says. "No one is good but God alone." (Luke 18:19) Throughout the gospels, the disciples and crowds want to lift Jesus' status, but he prevents them.

After healings and miracles, we hear Jesus say, "tell no one" (see Luke 5: 14 or Mark 9: 9). When Jesus asks the disciples who they think he is, Simon Peter answers, "You are the Messiah, the Son of the living God." (Matthew 16: 16) Jesus commends Simon Peter for his response, in the next breath ordering the disciples not to tell anyone.

What does it mean to say that Jesus was the Messiah?

Messiah literally means "Anointed one." For centuries before Jesus' birth, the Jewish people awaited a Messiah. Moses had freed the Israelites from slavery and oppression under Pharoah in Egypt. Now in the first century, the Jews believed a new anointed one would deliver their people after years of Roman oppression (and before Rome, Jewish people had suffered under other oppressors, including Babylon).

Prior to Jesus, Jewish prophets came one after another, drawing attention to Israel's flaws. Each in their different ways, these prophets pointed the Israelites to repent, reminding them to be faithful to their covenant with God.

The prophets of old spoke of a Messiah who would come and redeem the Israelite people. Anticipation rose each year as Roman oppression escalated.

The Jewish people believed that the coming Messiah would be a King, descended from the line of David. This King would rule over Israel and free the people from bondage. Many false prophets claiming to be Messiah came and went.

Along comes Jesus.

While false prophets spoke highly of themselves, Jesus ordered his followers to be quiet after they witnessed miracles.

People expected the Messiah to ride into Jerusalem on chariots of fire. Hailed as a new "King," Jesus made his triumphant entry into Jerusalem on a donkey.

The radical group of zealots sought to overthrow Rome by violence and would have happily welcomed Jesus as their charismatic leader. Jesus did not support violent tactics, and did not join their ranks. Jesus preached about the conquering power of love, not force or might.

Jesus taught his disciples to "turn the other cheek" (Matthew 5: 39). He said, "Whoever takes up the sword will perish by the sword." (Matthew 26:52) Jesus' life and teaching modeled eliminating oppression and bondage rooted in peace and nonviolence.

What kind of Messiah was this?

Jesus said that the last would be first, and the first last. He told his followers to be like little children.

Jesus obeyed religious law to a point. The religious authorities considered him a rabble-rouser, breaking strict rules about Sabbath and cleanliness, giving strange new ideas about God and life.

Jesus was not the type of Messiah the Jewish people were expecting. Still, some whose ears and eyes were open knew there was something special about this new teacher. Though following Jesus wasn't the acceptable thing to do in the sight of the religious authorities, some courageous few followed their heart, leaving everything to be in the presence of the rabbi Jesus.

I am inspired anew every time I encounter Jesus in the scriptures. In no other human being do I find such pure teaching of the road to peace, and such pure embodiment of that road.

In our current day, there are a lot of teachers in spirituality and self-help who preach one thing and do the opposite. Integrity is the sign of a pure teacher. It points to someone who has fully integrated what they teach. Jesus was one such person.

Jesus not only preached that we ought to love our enemies, but he lived this out, even unto death on a cross.

While washing his disciples' feet, Jesus taught that the greatest among us is the servant to all.

Jesus told parables about forgiveness while living out mercy to a degree that still blows my mind, forgiving those who hung him execution-style to die on a cross.

In Jesus, I see the fullest embodiment of a life lived in the light of God's love and peace. If all of us were to live as Jesus did, peace and harmony would reign supreme in our world today.

Jesus taught that change must begin within. Peace and love cannot be forced. They must come freely from the human heart. Look at what Jesus says about the importance of the heart:

— 'You shall love the Lord your God with all your heart, and with all your soul, and with all your mind.' This is the greatest and first commandment. (Matthew 22: 37-38)
— Blessed are the pure in heart, for they will see God. (Matthew 5: 8)
— For where your treasure is, there your heart will be also. (Matthew 6: 21)
— But what comes out of the mouth proceeds from the heart, and this is what defiles. For out of the heart come evil intentions, murder, adultery, fornication, theft, false witness,

slander. These are what defile a person, but to eat with unwashed hands does not defile." (Matthew 15: 18-20)

Jesus prayed that we may all be one (John 17: 21) and lived in such a way that would make that possible. Jesus taught a way of life, not strict doctrine. Strict doctrine out of alignment with love was what upset Jesus most.

Jesus' message was so clearly a way of life that the early Christian movement was known as "The Way."

Whenever the disciples tried to make things all about Jesus, Jesus pointed them back to God. The exception to this is the gospel of John. The synoptic gospels present a cohesive, consistent picture of the life of Jesus. John is the most mystical of the four gospels, the last gospel written historically, and according to scholars, the least historically reliable gospel.

Nevertheless, John's gospel contains powerful truths about the life and teachings of Jesus.

When we read John through the mystical lens in which it was written, we see that John's gospel is a powerful testimony of Jesus' oneness with God, and with us.

In the gospel of John Jesus quotes Psalm 82, saying, "Is it not written in your law, 'I said, you are gods'?" (John 10: 34)

The gospel of John contains all of the mystical "I am" statements of Jesus: "I am the gate" (John 10: 7, 9), "I am the bread of life" (John 6: 35), "I am the true vine" (John 15: 1), "I am the way, the truth, and the life" (John 14: 6), "I am the good shepherd" (John 10: 11), and "I am the light of the world" (John 8: 12)

These statements in John's gospel point to Jesus' oneness with God, which Christians believe is reflected in the Trinity: "On that day you will know that I am in my Father, and you in me, and I in you." (John 14: 20)

Jesus pointed us to <u>our own</u> oneness with God as much as to his. Jesus desired for us to see our own dormant divinity within. For this reason, Jesus said that not only was he the light of the world, but that "You are the light of the world." (Matthew 5: 14)

Jesus performed miracles and lived an extraordinary life of love and service. Perhaps even more extraordinarily, Jesus also said "Very truly, I tell you, the one who believes in me will also do the works that I do and, in fact, will do greater works than these (John 14: 12)

The Trinity does not exclude you and me. Rather, "As members of the mystical body, Christians actually partake in the divine nature of the Trinity."[45]

Jesus avoided being put on a pedestal because he knew that doing so would turn him into the ultimate exception, rather than the ultimate example, of how humans could live.

"Jesus Christ gradually became promoted in people's understanding from the status of a great spiritual master to someone higher than anything even imaginable: the Absolute Master, the 'only Son of God.'"[46]

Christians have often believed that "it is heresy to claim that we are as special as Jesus."[47] But could this be true? What if Jesus truly meant what he said- that we were to not only *strive* to live as he did, but that we actually *could*? What a monumental statement. Could humans be up for the task?

In Christian tradition, God became incarnate in the person of Jesus. Christian tradition says that Jesus was simultaneously fully human and fully divine. The implicit message of Christian teachings is that humans are fully human, while Jesus was supremely special and divine in a way that we humans could never be.

---

[45] McColman, Carl *The Big Book of Christian Mysticism: The Essential Guide to Contemplative Spirituality* (Charlottesville, VA: Hampton Roads Publishing Company, 2010), 165-166.

[46] Kriyananda, Swami, *Revelations of Christ Proclaimed by Paramhansa Yogananda*, (Nevada City, CA, Crystal Clarity Publishers, 2007), 14.

[47] Walsch, Neale Donald, *The New Revelations: A Conversation with God*, (New York, Atria Books, 2002), 89.

Did Jesus say that we were the light of the world as he was; did he teach that we could do even *greater* things than he, just to encourage us to live like he did, though we never really could? Did Jesus believe that humans could never really reach his heights or depths of spiritual attainment? If so, why did early church teachers make such bold claims as "Let the same mind be in you that was in Christ Jesus" (Philippians 2: 5) and "The gifts he gave were that some would be apostles, some prophets... until all of us come to the unity of the faith... to maturity, to the measure of the full stature of Christ." (Ephesians 4: 11-13)

What if Jesus was not the exclusive Son of God; the sole Anointed One? What if we are all Sons and Daughters of God, each with our own unique message and contribution to humanity? Surely each person's message will be unique, just as Jesus' life and message was unique. We cannot replicate Jesus' life, just as nobody else can replicate our life.

Jesus' message was the antithesis of a "superiority" gospel. Jesus did not proclaim himself superior to us in all things, that we might worship him as God and ourselves as unworthy sinners. Jesus proclaimed a Oneness gospel. In this new paradigm, we are One with Christ, One with God, and One with all of life. We only need wake up to this reality.

When we do, we realize that "Every human being is as special as every other human being who has ever lived, lives now, or ever will live. You are all messengers. Every one of you."[48] In the words of an anonymous Hopi elder, "We are the ones we've been waiting for." For peace to truly come to this world, we must begin living it ourselves. It starts with each one of us, right here, right now. As Rabbi Hillel famously said, "If not now, when? If not you, who?"

---

[48]   Walsch, Neale Donald, *The New Revelations: A Conversation with God*, (New York, Atria Books, 2002), 91-92.

CHAPTER TWELVE

SUBSTITUTIONARY SACRIFICIAL ATONEMENT

If you have not disagreed with me yet in this book- well, miracles happen! Each of us has our own unique perspective on faith. Some parts of this book may resonate with you, and some may challenge you. In some parts you may shout "Hallelujah!" and in others you may vehemently disagree. Don't worry, I won't take it personally. ☺

It is easy to talk about Oneness and unity when we agree with one another. It is much more difficult to manifest unity when we have strong disagreements! This is one of many reasons why I have great respect for the denomination I am ordained in, the United Church of Christ (UCC). The UCC so deeply valued Jesus' admonition "that they may all be one" (John 17: 21) that it underwent the difficult work of combining multiple denominations into one. Seeking to unite faith communities with a wide range of beliefs and liturgical practices is no small feat!

In unitive religious work, no matter what we believe or how strongly we disagree with one another, our first task is to embody the great commandment of love, as expressed in this prayer of Marco Antonio de Dominis:

> In essentials, unity,
> in nonessentials, liberty,
> in all things charity.

The difficultly integrating this prayer is knowing what is essential and what is not. On this very question do strong disagreements arise.

If in our disagreements we can remember above all to keep our hearts charitable, then we will not cease to love one another.

Even if you disagree with me in these pages, I hope I have made clear my intention to return Christianity to the love that Jesus preached and lived. The intent underlying this book is to give Christianity back to agape love in all things- in our words and actions, and in our thoughts and beliefs about God, Jesus, ourselves, and one another.

With that said, if you disagree with me on the next topic, no problem! For years I have struggled with my own theological questions, wrestling with Christian tradition while seeking to stay true with what resonates deep in my heart. I encourage you to do the same.

In my personal spiritual practice, listening to the heart is deeply connected to listening to the voice of God. Heart-centered listening does not mean that I follow every feeling that comes up without hesitation. Listening to the heart is a process of discernment where I seek to separate the still, small voice of God from the voice of the ego; the voice of love from the voice of fear; the voice of the soul from the negative voices of culture, family, and society.

In discernment, we pay close attention to how God is speaking to us today.

The theory of substitutionary sacrificial atonement articulated in classic Christian theology never sat quite right with my heart. Traditional Christian atonement theology begins with humans receiving a death sentence from God because of the sin of Adam and Eve. "When Adam and Eve broke God's law in the garden, they offended and angered God. So heinous was their crime that their punishment extended to all of humanity for all time. The antidote to this situation is the crucifixion of the Incarnate Son of God because only the suffering and death of an equally infinite and infallible being could ever satisfy the infinite offense of the infinitely dishonored God and assuage his wrath. Yikes!"[49]

According to this theory, Jesus' death was meant to pay the price for our sins. Jesus satisfied God's wrath and humanity's death sentence through his own death on a cross.

Many Christians find beauty and comfort in the idea that Jesus saves us from our own sinfulness. But I always wondered: what is the natural conclusion from this theory about the God whom Jesus loved?

The mixed theological message is this: "God wanted to destroy me, but Jesus had died for me. I found myself wishing God could be more like Jesus."[50]

Does it make sense that God- who created humans with free will- would sentence us to die for exercising that same will? As articulated by Doug Pagitt, "Jesus was not sent as the selected one to appease the anger of the Greek blood God. Jesus was sent to fulfill the promise of the Hebrew love God by ending human hostility. It was not the anger of God that Jesus came to end but the anger of people."[51]

All this begs the question, "Why must sins be paid for? If God is forgiving, why is any payment necessary?"[52]

In the days of Jesus, Jewish people went to the temple in Jerusalem to offer animal sacrifices to God. These blood sacrifices

---

[49]   Pagitt, Doug, *A Christianity Worth Believing: Hope-Filled, Open-Armed, Alive-And-Well Faith*, (San Francisco, Jossey-Bass, 2008), 154.

[50]   Gulley P & Mulholland J., *If Grace is True: Why God Will Save Every Person*, (New York, HarperOne, 2003), 9.

[51]   Pagitt, Doug, *A Christianity Worth Believing: Hope-Filled, Open-Armed, Alive-And-Well Faith*, (San Francisco, Jossey-Bass, 2008), 194.

[52]   Gulley P & Mulholland J., *If Grace is True: Why God Will Save Every Person*, (New York, HarperOne, 2003), 127.

were a gift from the human to the divine, which in turn removed sin and brought blessings. As John Dominic Crossan articulates, "You get the gods attention with a gift/sacrifice. Nobody thinks, 'We really deserve to be put to death, but we'll take it out on the sheep.' The sacrifice functioned as a gift."[53]

Early Christians retold this ritual and narrative, reframing sacrifice so that faithful Jews could embrace the path of Jesus. In this reframing, Jews no longer needed to offer animal sacrifices as a means of purifying their sin. Instead, Jesus was the last and final sacrifice; the sacrifice to end all sacrifices. Through his blood, and not the blood of any animal, sins were forgiven.

Early Christians retelling of the story of Jesus transformed the meaning of sacrifice.

Substitutionary sacrificial atonement theory was first articulated centuries later by Anselm, the Archbishop of Canterbury. In the 11th century, Anselm's reasoning went like this: God is a just judge. No judge can say in a courtroom, "You're all forgiven." That judge would be impeached. If God cares about us, there must be a punishment for our sin. Instead, God sends his son to be an adequate victim in our place.[54]

Plenty of scripture passages can be used to justify viewing God as a judge. However, if we take our cues from Jesus' life and ministry, then scripture is not our ultimate authority. Love is. Whenever scripture or tradition were out of alignment with love, Jesus challenged them.

We must ask of any scripture or church tradition if it is in alignment with love. If it is, keep it; if not, let it go. As articulated by the professor of theology I had in seminary: "A theology that has the heavenly Father punish his innocent Son to redeem the world looks uncomfortably to some like a charter for child abuse, with an

---

[53] Crossan, John Dominic, *Lecture at Awakenings Conference*, (Holyoke, MA, April 2014).

[54] Crossan, John Dominic, *Lecture at Awakenings Conference*, (Holyoke, MA, April 2014).

innocent son sent to bear the wrath of a "heavenly father" to make things right for the entire extended family."[55]

There is wisdom in the image of God as judge. This image can help us remember accountability for our actions, and inspire us to be more charitable. People who've had near-death-experiences (NDEs) often report having "life reviews" in the spiritual realm. In these life reviews, NDE experiencers relive the ways they both helped *and* harmed other people- experiencing the joy as well as the suffering caused to others.

This is the experience that we are all truly One- what we do to another, we do to ourselves.

That the Creator would structure a life review into the afterlife says a lot about the nature of God. It says that even after we leave our physical bodies, God cares about our growth. Just as any good parent wants their child to learn from their mistakes, God is no different. God wants to celebrate and lift up our successes, and help us avoid the mistakes that keep us locked in fear, prejudice, or violence.

This view of God as judge is radically different than the view portrayed by church tradition and articulated in classic atonement theology. The God of sacrificial atonement is a punishing Judge whose wrath must be appeased. Yet is the God of sacrificial atonement the same God of agape love we see expressed in and through the life of Jesus?

"The specific ways Christians have understood the cross often involve transactional analogies of substitution, ransom, or satisfaction... Such categories explain Jesus' death, but in such a way as to pose further troubling questions. If a debt is owed to God, why can't God simply forgive it, as Jesus apparently counsels others to do? If God is ransoming us from other powers, why does God have to submit to their terms? If this is God's wise and compassionate plan for salvation, why does it require such violence? ... We can hardly

---

[55] Heim, S. Mark, *Saved from Sacrifice: A Theology of the Cross* (Grand Rapids, Eerdmans Publishing Co., 2006), 25-26.

imagine God demanding the suffering and death of one innocent as the condition of mercy toward guilty others."[56]

The God of Agape love is a loving parent who always seeks our best, providing opportunities (in life and in death) for us to learn and grow into the persons we are called to be.

Jesus, a visible manifestation of the invisible God, sought to give all people back to love. Jesus sought to reframe traditions and beliefs that had lost sight of their essential spiritual purpose, love. Jesus invites us to view scripture and church tradition with the same critical eye as he did. Through this critical lens, we can ask whether beliefs or doctrines align with love.

Jesus' death on the cross was the ultimate sacrifice of love. Seeing the human condition of fear and violence, Jesus gave his life non-violently, in order that we might live another way. Jesus gave his life to show us the way to abundant life. In modeling the path of nonviolence and unconditional love, Jesus forgave even his persecutors after they had nailed him to die on a cross.

This love is the highest example of sacrifice; of laying down one's life for one's friends. In willingly undergoing death, Jesus hoped that we, like him, might experience resurrection and new life.

Like Jesus, we are called to question and rearticulate church scripture and tradition, so that these authorities might serve the highest goal of unconditional love.

Atonement, framed in another way, is At-One-Ment- honoring our Oneness with God, one another, and all creation. It was for this Oneness that Jesus died, both because of our sins, and to eradicate our sins.

There is another meaning to Jesus dying for our sins which saints attest to. Paramhansa Yogananda relates of his Self-Realized

---

56   Heim, S. Mark, *Saved from Sacrifice: A Theology of the Cross* (Grand Rapids, Eerdmans Publishing Co., 2006), 25.

guru, "Sri Yukteswar burned many of their (his disciples) sins in the fire of his severe fever in Kashmir."[57]

Burning the sins of disciples?!

I cannot speak from personal experience, because taking on another's sin/karma is outside of my spiritual toolbox. Nevertheless, the other day my 18-month-old daughter was not feeling good with a fever. As our minds tend to do, I began to think of the worst-case scenario. Desiring my daughter's health above my own, I prayed, "Lord, if I can take this pain in her stead, I'd be glad to. Please, give me her suffering."

Such great love do I have for my daughter that without hesitation I would sacrifice my health for her benefit. Any parent who has touched that inexhaustible love for their child has felt the same, asking "How can I take their pain away?"

If I, an unenlightened seeker, want to relieve another's karma, wouldn't an enlightened being (who feels boundless love for all) want to take away the karmic pains of their disciples?

Hypothetically, if a saint free of negative karma could ease their disciple's karma by sacrificing themselves or their health, what's to prevent them? Being Self-Realized, they are free of remaining karma to work out. Might not these enlightened saints desire to take on their disciple's karma and ease their spiritual burdens? After all, each saint only lives physically for a time. Future generations will learn their spiritual teachings through disciples. As Yogananda shares, "The metaphysical method of physical transfer of disease is known to highly advanced yogis. A strong man can assist a weaker one by helping to carry his heavy load; a spiritual superman is able to minimize his disciples' physical or mental burdens by sharing the karma of their past actions. Just as a rich man loses some money when he pays off a large debt for his prodigal son, who is thus saved from dire consequences of his own folly, so a master willingly

---

[57]   Yogananda, Paramhansa, *Autobiography of a Yogi*, (Crystal Clarity Publishers, https://www.ananda.org/autobiography), Chapter 21.

sacrifices a portion of his bodily wealth to lighten the misery of disciples."[58]

Yogananda describes the process: "By a secret method, the yogi unites his mind and astral vehicle with those of a suffering individual; the disease is conveyed, wholly or in part, to the saint's body. Having harvested God on the physical field, a master no longer cares what happens to that material form. Though he may allow it to register a certain disease in order to relieve others, his mind is never affected; he considers himself fortunate in being able to render such aid."[59]

Asserting that Jesus' death takes away humanity's sins and negative karma for all time does not align with spiritual principles. One person's death cannot take away the sins of the whole world for eternity. Look at civilization after Jesus' death and resurrection. Society didn't get less violent and destructive, but more so!

At the same time, we must remember that divine grace is always forgiving when we err. It is love most of all- divine or human- that releases us from error, ignorance, and sin. Peter, one of Jesus' closest disciples, speaks from experience about the freeing power of love: "Above all, maintain constant love for one another, for love covers a multitude of sins." (1 Peter 4: 8)

Jesus conveys to his disciples the significance of his sacrifice on the cross soon before the crucifixion: "No one has greater love than this, to lay down one's life for one's friends." (John 15: 13)

May we embody this vision, lived out by Jesus, and articulated by the early Christians: "Dear friends, let us love one another...for love comes from God. Whoever loves is born of God...for God is love...")! (1 John 4:7-8)

---

58   Yogananda, Paramhansa, *Autobiography of a Yogi*, (Crystal Clarity Publishers, https://www.ananda.org/autobiography), Chapter 21.

59   Yogananda, Paramhansa, *Autobiography of a Yogi*, (Crystal Clarity Publishers, https://www.ananda.org/autobiography), Chapter 21.

CHAPTER THIRTEEN

DEATH AND RESURRECTION, BEING BORN AGAIN

Currently in human history, darkness seems to be increasing throughout our world. Since the Trump administration took power in 2017, hate groups in the U.S. have felt more emboldened than ever to spread messages of fear, bigotry, and prejudice. Hate crimes spiked to an all-time high during the Trump Presidency. What to do about this disturbing trend?

Spiritually speaking, two principles are at work here. First, many spiritual teachers affirm that we are at a unique juncture in spiritual history. More light is breaking into our world than ever before. Spiritual transformation is happening at an unprecedented rate.

The other principle happening simultaneously may seem to be at odds with the expansive light breaking into our lives. This principle has been called many things, including "The Law of Opposites." The Law of Opposites relates that as more love comes into the world, more fear comes up also.

On a personal level, this is at work whenever we declare ourselves to be anything. "I am peace!" "I am love" "I am light!"

As soon as we make these declarations, we often notice that more of the opposite comes into our lives- stress, anxiety, and fear. What's going on?

On the surface this may feel like bad news, and to the ego it is. At the surface, nobody wants more fear in life. Who wants a "dark night of the soul?"

Paradoxically, these dark nights can be the opportunities for our greatest spiritual growth. We declare ourselves to be love, and fear comes up. We express wanting more peace in the world and in our life, and yet anxiety, stress, and violence take an ever-greater hold.

The good news is that the opposite comes up precisely to be released.

Saying that we want more love in our lives and in the world is a first step. Love wants to break in, but if our hearts are already full (with desires, attachments, fears) then we won't be able to receive that love fully.

To create space, the fear that lies hidden in our subconscious must be transmuted. Fear and violence come up to our conscious awareness to be released.

So long as our fears remain buried within the subconscious, they have a hidden power over us. Once we recognize that they exist, we begin the work of transformation.

The post-2016 Presidential election reality is a simple example. Since that election, racism has reared its head in the U.S. in ugly ways. People and groups who promote fear and prejudice feel emboldened in their actions. Prior to this emboldening, many people assumed that the U.S. was a post-racial society, and that racism had been done away with during the civil rights movement of the 1960s.

It has become crystal clear for those with eyes to see that race is an issue that needs attention and healing in our society. What appeared hidden to those with privilege can no longer be denied.

Too often when forms of "negativity" arise in our life, they are seen as problems best dealt with through ignorance, denial, or suppression.

Ignoring, denying, or suppressing a problem does not lead to a solution.

It is interesting that "every living being feels its fear and shakes it off. Cows, deer, fox, even bears- they all feel fear and move on. But we human beings don't. We accumulate fear. We hoard and store it in our bodies... And then it keeps us locked into place."[60]

Many people still deny the reality of racism or other forms of negativity that exist in our lives and in the world. Denial is one way that the ego clings to its perception of reality.

Acceptance of what is is the beginning of the end for our distorted ego. So long as we pretend that our distorted perceptions are true, the grasp of the ego maintains its hold on us.

To practice resurrection is to continually die to our egoic self and be reborn into life in the Spirit. This is a practice, not a one-time event. Rebirth is something we open to continually as we grow in our work, our relationships, and our aspirations.

We must be cautious if we ever think we have fully "arrived" spiritually. There are ever-expanding levels of growth. Each time we proclaim that we are light or love, something will come up in us to be released.

We spend our childhood and much of our adult lives developing a healthy ego. The goal of spiritual progress, perhaps paradoxically, is to die to ego-identification and identify ever-increasingly with Spirit. This is a lifelong process because our ego likes to be in control and puts up a good fight to stay in the driver's seat.

Jesus, like us, had to overcome his ego. After being baptized by John, Jesus went to the desert to overcome any last vestiges of egoic identification with worldly power and prestige.

During this intense 40 days of fasting and purification in the desert, Jesus was tempted with all the kingdoms of the world- a sweet deal to the ego. Being deeply attuned to Spirit, Jesus knew that material things are passing and that our ultimate identity is in God. From this place of Self-Realization, Jesus replied in the face

---

[60] Desai, Panache, *Discovering Your Soul Signature: A 33-Day Path to Purpose, Passion & Joy*, (New York, Random House, 2014), 4.

of temptation, "Worship the Lord your God, and serve only Him." (Matthew 4: 10)

The ego finds its identification with wealth, power, and material things, but also in belief systems and ideologies. This is evident in how frequently political and religious belief structures have been used to marginalize, hurt, and oppress.

Spiritual liberation does not come from a belief system. Our freedom in God comes through spiritual experience.

Belief is knowledge about; experience is direct knowing. Beliefs can be ephemeral and hurtful and change over time. Experience of God is transformative and eternal. Anyone who experiences God is always transformed in the direction of love because God is love.

One of the church's great examples is Saul (who is later renamed Paul). Saul was an expert in using spiritual law and belief to hurt and oppress Jesus' disciples. While on the road to Damascus, Saul is blinded, confronted with his egoic, harmful approach to religion. Jesus asks directly, "Saul, Saul, why are you persecuting me?"

Though Saul had a wealth of knowledge about the law, he was lacking in spiritual experience. Saul knew a lot about God but had never directly encountered God. In his experience on the Damascus road, Saul is immediately transformed.

For three days, Saul remains blind, sitting with the knowledge of how much pain and suffering he had caused from a place of spiritual blindness. Paul's direct experience of God is a catalyst for transformation.

In John 3: 3, Jesus says, 'Very truly, I tell you, no one can see the kingdom of God without being born again.'

In many Christian circles, being "born again" is associated with belief, a form of intellectual assent. To determine if someone has been "born again," Christians commonly ask: "Do you believe in Jesus as your Lord and Savior?" or "Have you accepted Jesus Christ as your Lord and Savior?"

What if being born again was not about belief, but total life transformation?

Paul, formerly Saul, knows about total life transformation more than anyone. Having lived it firsthand, Paul can say in the words of John Newton, "I once was lost, but now am found; was blind, but now I see." From that experience, Paul says, "Do you not know that all of us who have been baptized into Christ Jesus were baptized into his death? Therefore we have been buried with him by baptism into death, so that, just as Christ was raised from the dead by the glory of the Father, so we too might walk in newness of life. For if we have been united with him in a death like his, we will certainly be united with him in a resurrection like his. We know that our old self was crucified with him so that the body of sin might be destroyed, and we might no longer be enslaved to sin. For whoever has died is freed from sin." (Romans 6: 3-7)

God is always with us. Only our fears, insecurities, and unwholesome habits blind us to this reality. In being "born again," we experience a metaphorical "death" to all that does not serve us on the spiritual path- to fear, prejudice, bitterness, greed, apathy, lust, needing to control others, addiction, rage, and so on.

Being born again does not mean denying or suppressing our feelings. Rather, by first accepting our negative feelings, they can move through us, and we are emptied to begin anew.

Grief is a spot-on example. Much of North American culture values grief in theory, but not in practice. We do not allow ourselves to feel the deep sadness in losses we experience. Instead, we project that sadness onto the loved ones in our life.

This, of course, just touches the surface. Grief manifests in countless unwholesome ways when not dealt with through healthy channels.

As a result of not allowing ourselves to feel our grief, we never move past it.

There is no way past grief except through it. In allowing ourselves to grieve- in our own time and in our own way- we let the grief pass through us.

Feeling our feelings can be a difficult practice to integrate, particularly when we've been taught to "tough it out." We can spend lifetimes in avoidance! This is why it is helpful to have the support of therapists, coaches, spiritual directors, spiritual companions, or spiritual community. Small groups and retreats can also bring healing.

Sometimes we need to forgive others. Much of the time we need to forgive ourselves.

The scriptures say that Jesus, in becoming human, "emptied himself." (Philippians 2: 7) In becoming like Christ, we too must be emptied. To live in and fill ourselves with God, we must first empty ourselves of ego and all that is not love.

Full of our own thoughts and opinions, we squeeze out God. To start afresh, we must empty ourselves of all that we think we are. As empty vessels, we become clear instruments for God's love to move through. In the words of the poet Hafiz, "I am a hole in a flute that the Christ's breath moves through...listen to this music."

This is the goal of the spiritual path- not only to emulate Jesus, but to tap into the Christ-consciousness: "Let the same mind be in you that was in Christ Jesus." (Philippians 2: 5)

Emptying happens on personal, interpersonal, and institutional levels. On personal and interpersonal levels, we empty ourselves of fear, and fill ourselves with love. As 1 John 4: 18 says, "perfect love casts out fear." This is a practice, not a one-time occurrence.

On institutional levels, emptying means purging fear, greed, prejudice, and violence from organizations and corporations-dismantling racism and prejudice against people of different races, sexual orientations, colors, ethnicities, gender identities and expressions, nationalities, socio-economic backgrounds, religions, and much more.

Corporations rooted in ego seek to expand material gain rather than spiritual awareness. On large and small scales, we are called to purify our culture's materialistic, ego-first mindset that consistently puts profits over people.

Being rooted in ego over soul-awareness leads to unsustainable practices that has already had devastating effects for present and future generations on our planet.

In waking up to who we truly are, we may grieve the loss of old ways of life, like the addict who struggles to be free of addiction. Yet in death to our old self, we experience newfound freedom.

This freedom comes as we realize at a deep level our Oneness with all people and all things. From that realization, we express Oneness in our work, our families, and our relationships.

In Self-realization, we live in the love that we are. In such a state, we could never consciously harm other humans or our fragile Earth.

"Then you will know the truth, and the truth will set you free." (John 8: 32)

Scripture uses the metaphor of sleep to point out our old, egoic self, blinded by fears and selfish gain. The prophet Isaiah uses the metaphors of sleep and bondage together: "Awake, awake, put on your strength, O Zion... Shake yourself from the dust, rise up, O captive Jerusalem; loose the bonds from your neck." (Isaiah 52: 1-2) When we experience the truth of who we are, we awaken from our long slumber.

In the letter to the Ephesian community, the author implores the church to be transformed: "For once you were darkness, but now in the Lord you are light. Live as children of light— for the fruit of the light is found in all that is good and right and true... Take no part in the unfruitful works of darkness, but instead expose them... everything exposed by the light becomes visible, for everything that becomes visible is light. Therefore it says, 'Sleeper, awake! Rise from the dead, and Christ will shine on you.' (Ephesians 5: 8-9, 11, 13-14)

Sleeper, awake! Be transformed!

Prophets and saints of all religions call us to transformation from sleeping to waking; from death to new life; from bondage to freedom. There is a personal dimension to this transformation, the first step. Personal transformation then inspires us to transform oppressive structures and institutions, including the Christian ones.

Jesus reserved some of his strongest words for the religious authorities of his time. Since Christianity became the religion of the Roman Empire, it has been in a constant struggle to return to the simplicity of the faith of Jesus. For centuries, the church has become caught in power struggles, fear-based violence, and preoccupation with belief, doctrine, and dogma.

During every historic age, the church has drifted further away from Jesus. This includes the 21st century church. We live in a time where most young people outside the church find Christians to be judgmental, hypocritical, anti-gay, and out-of-touch with reality.

The church has much to shed when people do not find Jesus in the church or Christ in the Christians.

A quick overview of Christian history highlights the church's long-standing intolerance and violence towards those who haven't accepted church doctrines or dogmas.

The good news of the gospel is that death and violence is never the last word.

In a time when churches of every stripe are declining and dying, what is God up to? Many church historians say that every 500 years, the church moves so far away from the core message of Jesus, it is compelled to hold a giant rummage sale. Anglican bishop Mark Dyer puts it this way: "Every 500 years or so the Church feels compelled to hold a giant rummage sale, and 'the empowered structures of institutionalized Christianity, whatever they may be at the time, become an intolerable carapace that must be shattered in order that renewal and new growth may occur.'"[61]

If individuals, society, and the church are to be life-giving, we must be born anew. This means "dying to an old way of being and being born into a new way of being, dying to an old identity and being born into a new identity- a new way of being and an identity centered in the sacred, in Spirit, in Christ, in God."[62]

---

[61] Tickle, Phyllis, *The Great Emergence: How Christianity Is Changing and Why*, (Grand Rapids, BakerBooks, 2008), 16.

[62] Borg, Marcus, *The Heart of Christianity: Rediscovering a Life of Faith*, (New York, HarperCollins, 2003), 107.

CHAPTER FOURTEEN

EMBODYING THE GOOD NEWS: SPIRITUAL COMMUNITY & BEING CONTEMPLATES IN ACTION

Have you ever felt that life never seem to slow down, but seems to move at a breakneck pace?

The pace of our lives IS increasing. With more things to do, and technology ever-increasing, there are more things to keep track of than we are able to. The sheer speed of life and the magnitude of our responsibilities can exhaust and overwhelm us.

I know this is true for myself as well. As the scope of my ministries has increased, and as my family has expanded (to have a beautiful daughter), I've found it progressively more challenging to keep a balance between work, family, exercise, rest, and time for spiritual practices.

My wife LaToya is from Belize, a small country in Central America. I love Belize. Though Belizean people are busy too, there is a slower pace and a more relaxed atmosphere that pervades Belizean culture. Whenever I travel to Belize, I am reminded of my need for balance. Living in Massachusetts, I often get pulled too far in the direction of overwork, stress, and worry that our culture reinforces.

Having grown up outside of Boston, I know that Massachusetts life is commonly lived at a frantic, rather than a sacred, pace.

The apostle Paul says in Romans 7: 15: "I do not understand my own actions. For I do not do what I want, but I do the very thing I hate." I have found Paul's statement true for me also. Why is it easier to be relaxed in Belize? Why is it easier to fall into a fast-paced frenzy when I'm in Boston? Mere coincidence?

The Indian saint Paramhansa Yogananda often said, "environment in stronger than will power."

Each of us are influenced, knowingly or not, by the culture around us. The communities surrounding us and the positive or negative vibrations they emit influence our state of being.

That is why community is so important on the spiritual path. If we can be part of life-giving communities that model a different way of being, then we can begin to counteract the negative influences of our culture and our world.

There are many reasons why people who are spiritual shy away from spiritual community. Many have been scarred by religious communities and are reluctant to try again. Many have searched but been unable to find a community that resonates with them- a place where they are fed spiritually.

My calling to ministry has led me in the direction of creating spiritual community that feeds people's souls. One way I love doing this is through retreats. When people feel safe at retreats, they allow themselves to be real and vulnerable. As a result, the sharing, reflection, prayer, Sabbath, and cup-filling can be magnificent. To be at a transformational retreat is to experience the creation of life-giving, soul-feeding community.

More recently, I have felt called to create community not only through retreats, but through starting a new spiritual community in Waltham, Massachusetts called "Agape Spiritual Community."

One scripture that deeply informs how I view community and the spiritual life is from this passage from the gospel of Luke: "Now during those days he [Jesus] went out to the mountain to pray;

and he spent the night in prayer to God. And when day came, he called his disciples and chose twelve of them, whom he also named apostles…

"He came down with them and stood on a level place, with a great crowd of his disciples and a great multitude of people from all Judea, Jerusalem, and the coast of Tyre and Sidon. They had come to hear him and to be healed of their diseases; and those who were troubled with unclean spirits were cured. And all in the crowd were trying to touch him, for power came out from him and healed all of them." (Luke 6: 12-13, 17-19)

There are three movements in this passage central to the spiritual life. The first is the contemplative one. Jesus spends the night in prayer to God. Throughout Jesus' life, he prioritizes his relationship with God by spending time in prayer and meditation to fill his cup.

Jesus was human, like the rest of us. He got tired and worn down from the fullness of life and ministry, just like the rest of us. In the gospels we often read about Jesus going off to find a quiet, solitary place to rest and to pray.

Contemplation points to the mystical dimension of faith, where we engage in spiritual practices that connect us to the divine.

In today's world, we are so "go-go-go" all the time that we have difficulty relaxing and simply being. When we are always in the habit of do-do-do and go-go-go, our minds never rest from productive activity.

People who go on vacation often have difficulty unplugging and relaxing when they are supposed to NOT do anything. I have known newly retired persons who, prior to retirement, rarely carved out intentional times of solitude, rest, or refreshment. In the absence of work, they literally don't know what to DO with themselves! Their whole lives up to that point were a practice of doing, with little to no practice in being.

During seminary, I took a course entitled "Spiritual Practices for Healing and Wholeness" for a semester. One assignment for the class was to practice regularly one new spiritual discipline. I was intrigued by the practice of Sabbath in the Jewish and Christian traditions and decided to keep a Sabbath practice over the course of the semester.

By taking scheduled time to rest, restore, and renew, I found at the end of the semester that I had more energy for the tasks of ministry, which at times can be very demanding. In taking time to care for my own soul, I found that my spiritual cup was filled. I was able to give to others from a full, instead of an empty, place. To this day, I still have a weekly Sabbath practice where I take time out to rest, spend time with family, and connect with God through spiritual practices.

Though I do not read all biblical stories literally, I do see great spiritual truth in the creation stories of the Bible. The book of Genesis says that after six days of creating, God rested on the seventh day. The spiritual message behind the story is clear- if even God rested after work, how much more must we!

For most of us, taking the time to rest our bodies, minds, and souls amid our busy lives is not laziness or idleness. It is, I dare say, a necessity. To constantly push ourselves without rest, renewal, and refreshment leads to high levels of stress, overwhelm, and burnout.

Time for God, spiritual practice, family, rest and community is not selfish. On the contrary, it is what one of my favorite professors from seminary Rev. Dr. Kirk Jones calls "self-is-ness." It is time that we carve out to nurture and sustain our sacred self.

Self-ish-ness harms others and stems from greed. Self-is-ness benefits others and stems from self-love.

Self-love is one of the most important parts of Jesus' great commandment, and yet is often overlooked! When Jesus was asked what the "greatest commandment" was, he responded, "to love God with all your heart, soul, mind, and strength, and to love your neighbor as you love yourself."

The second half of this commandment- to love others as we love ourselves- includes the imperative to love ourselves! Without a healthy love of ourselves, we won't have a healthy love for others. Healthy self-love is the foundation for loving others.

The book "Dying To Be Me" by Anita Moorjani is a powerful account of Anita's near-death-experience and all that she learned travelling to the "other side." Anita's account speaks beautifully to the power of self-love:

"People ask me whether there's such a thing as too much self-love. Where's the line, they ask, where it starts to become selfish or egotistical? To me, there's no such possibility. There is no line. Selfishness comes from lack of self-love. Our planet is suffering from this, as we humans are, along with too much insecurity, judgment, and conditioning. In order to truly care for someone unconditionally, I have to feel that way toward myself. I can't give away what I don't have."[63]

Self-love is what Jesus did when he went off to the mountain to pray. Even more than self-love, he loved the Source of all being, what some of us call God.

There are many ways to connect to the Divine. I dare say there are as many spiritual exercises as there are physical exercises to choose from!

To become physically fit, it doesn't matter so much what form our physical exercise takes. Similarly with spiritual exercise, it doesn't matter what form our spiritual exercises takes. What matters is that we do them!

Physical exercises keep our body healthy; spiritual exercises keep our soul healthy. As body, mind, and spirit are One, any form of mental, emotional, or spiritual exercise will have a positive impact on the WHOLE of us!

After spending the night in prayer to God, Jesus comes down from the mountain and gathers a community. This is the second important movement in the spiritual life. Jesus had times of retreat and meditation by himself (remember the intensive 40 days

---

[63] Moorjani, Anita, *Dying To Be Me: My Journey From Cancer, To Near Death, to True Healing*, (New York City, Hay House, 2012), 139-140.

of fasting!), but he started his ministry by forming community around him.

In United States culture today, we place a high value on autonomy. Henri Nouwen, a beloved author and Catholic priest, shared in his writings how his own individualism and desire for personal success "ever and again tempt me to do it alone and to claim the task of ministry for myself. But Jesus didn't preach and heal alone."[64]

If you don't feel that you have a spiritual community that nurtures you, I invite you to risk the search for one. It will be a risk, just like dating is a risk. The reward of dating is to find another whom you love and can share your life with. The reward of searching for life-giving spiritual community is having others whom you love spiritually (in a non-romantic way :) and can share your spiritual life with.

If no communities in your area resonate with you spiritually, look for communities that you can connect to by phone, virtually, or occasionally in person. In the words of Yvette Flunder, "We join faith communities to be strengthened and nurtured and to have an opportunity to serve. When these goals are no longer attainable, we should look elsewhere."[65]

Unfortunately, many people have experienced deep wounds in churches and spiritual communities. The brokenness of humanity is not absent from church. Church, just like any community, is messy. Church can test our faith and our patience. While no community is perfect, "We need to remain aware of systems, churches, and communities that breed none of the openness that is in God. Church should not be hazardous to your health. Spirituality should not take from you... Relationships and communities are meant to be places

---

64   Nouwen, Henri: *Henri Nouwen: Writings Selected With an Introduction by Robert A. Jonas*, (New York, Orbis Books, 1998), 97.

65   Flunder, Yvette: *Where the Edge Gathers: Building a Community of Radical Inclusion*, (Cleveland, The Pilgrim Press, 2005), p. 23.

where people build one another up in faith and love, places for us to be seen and to see others."[66]

After spending the night in prayer to God and gathering community in the morning, Jesus goes to the crowds to teach and to heal. This is the third movement: the ministry of making God's love and justice real in the world; working for "Thy kingdom come." The kingdom of God, Jesus said, is at hand, here and now (see Mark 1: 15). Not only is it among us, it is also within every one of us, lest we search high and low and not inside ourselves. (See Luke 17: 21)

We live into the kingdom of God every time we give to a neighbor in need. The kingdom of God is expanded every time we see the divinity in another, and every time we reach out to someone in compassionate care. This kingdom is one of love and of justice. It invites us to work for change in society on multiple levels.

Living into this kingdom means first re-orienting our hearts towards love. A good news centered heart moves deeper into love, as God's perfect love casts out fear.

The more we are intentional about living in God, the more we will expand our love of self, our love of others, and our love of all creation.

Changing our heart leads to changes in our interpersonal relationships, where we seek to live out the fruits of the spirit in Galatians 5: 22-23: love, peace, joy, patience, kindness, generosity, faithfulness, gentleness, and self-control.

When we care about God's kingdom, living in this transformed way becomes our first priority.

For me, a changed heart led to re-orienting my life towards service and social justice. This sometimes looks like serving and cooking at a homeless shelter, or just as important, accompanying and listening to the stories of the people I serve. In whatever way this happens, my life no longer revolves around my needs alone.

---

[66] Pagitt, Doug: *Flipped: The Provocative Truth That Changes Everything We Know About God*, (New York, Convergent Books, 2015), 203-204.

Justice invites me to serve others not only through charity, but through advocacy. Someone needs a meal today, and it is important to provide that. But justice asks the questions: "Why are hunger and homelessness major issues in our society today?" "What issues, policies, and larger societal structures can I change that will make it easier for those on the margins to access jobs, housing and transportation?"

These questions do not have simple answers. Since the solutions to these questions don't come overnight, it is important to do the work of charity while we seek justice.

Asking why someone is hungry or homeless connects to many other social justice questions related to race, education, and the environment, to name a few. For example, why are schools with children of color overwhelmingly less well-resourced than suburban schools composed mostly of white children? Why is there such a high incarceration rate among black and Hispanic youth and adults?

People of color, persons on the margins, and persons who are lower on the socio-economic scale are more adversely affected by the increased natural disasters resulting from climate change. In a time when our dependence on fossil fuels is damaging our planet and hurting the most vulnerable among us, how are we invited to change our lifestyles? How can we impact change at a corporate level, where too often profits are placed before people and the earth?

These are all big questions, with answers that are even bigger and more far-reaching. Because these questions and realities can be overwhelming, it's even more important to follow in the example of Jesus.

Jesus' movement in faith was to take time for solitude and spiritual practice; to form and be sustained by spiritual community; and go change the world. The order of that movement is important. When I first moved from service to activism in my college years, I met a lot of people working for peace in the world who were not peaceful inside themselves. They appeared more burned out and ego-identified than calm, loving, and emotionally grounded.

When we work to change the world from a foundation of faith, we know that we do not go it alone. We are supported by the love and presence of the Divine, and by the love and presence of like-minded, faith-filled people. We can't do it alone, and we shouldn't.

I know I can get overwhelmed thinking about the magnitude of injustice in the world. What keeps me faithful is knowing that I am not alone. I walk with other co-conspirators in this work of love and justice.

The world may not change as quickly as we would like. The kind of structural changes suggested here do not come about until there is adequate political will- a sufficient change in heart. People need to care about something for motion to happen. Even then, change is gradual. We do not change the entire world overnight. In the words of a prayer by Bishop Kenneth Untener, often attributed to Oscar Romero,

> No program accomplishes the church's mission.
> No set of goals and objectives includes everything.
> We plant the seeds that one day will grow.
> We lay foundations that will need further development.
> We cannot do everything, and there is a sense of liberation in realizing that.
> We may never see the end results, but that is the difference between the master builder and the worker.
> We are workers, not master builders; ministers, not messiahs.
> We are prophets of a future not our own. Amen.

CHAPTER FIFTEEN

SPIRITUAL GIFTS AND OVERCOMING EGO

For as long as church has been church, spiritual communities have identified and affirmed people's innate divine gifts. One of my favorite scriptures in 1 Corinthians 12 points out that we are one body and many members. As all of us are different, we all have gifts that differ accordingly. Paul writes, "Now there are varieties of gifts, but the same Spirit; and there are varieties of activities, but it is the same God who activates all of them in everyone. To each is given the manifestation of the Spirit for the common good." (1 Corinthians 12: 4-6)

In principle, church teaches that all gifts are equal. In practice, some gifts are regarded as spiritually superior. Take being "set apart" as Clergy for the ministry of Word and Sacrament. This gift has been elevated to the highest service one can render God through our gifts.

Being "chosen by God," people look at and treat you differently. Special favors are sought out. In these circumstances, it is common to let power, prestige, or reputation go to your head. In times like these, ego gets the best of us.

Clergy may start the road to ministry using our gifts and following our calling with a noble heart. Yet the slippery slope of praise and power too often causes us to give priority to our own egos and small circles of care.

This trajectory is not unique to ministry. It can be seen in public service of all forms, politics especially. Many newcomers start their political journey with a good heart and sincere ambitions to help others. However, the temptation to uplift oneself is easily within reach, and the pedestal raising from others frequently becomes the expected norm.

Spiritually speaking, many gifts aren't treated equally, and many are even looked down upon, including gifts Jesus expressed in his life and ministry. Gifts of clairvoyance, clairaudience, or claircognizance, for example, are often met with suspicion. Many churchgoers lump these gifts into the "woo-woo" category. And yet, the ability to peer into future realities was demonstrated many times by Jesus, as we see in the gospels.

What has changed from Jesus' day to ours? Unfortunately, many "quacks"- people who misrepresent themselves and their gifts to others seeking spiritual help- get the most public attention. Also too common is people with authentic spiritual gifts who put money first, above the welfare of others.

Nevertheless, many psychics, healers, mediums, or intuitives do not put the almighty dollar first. Many have accepted their God-given gifts with grace and humility, putting God first in a spirit of selfless service.

This is how Jesus invites us to hold whatever gifts are present in our spiritual lives.

If we are to grow spiritually, then our unique talents are meant to be shared with others. In the case of communicating with loved ones who have "passed on," this gift has long been demonized and vilified within spiritual circles.

There is a story in the Hebrew Bible that speaks to our long-standing tension around spiritual gifts considered "occult." In the latter days of Saul being king, Saul began to lose favor with God. Though Saul was desperate for spiritual advice, his advisor Samuel had recently died. Ironically, Saul had outlawed all mediums in the land. Nonetheless, Saul told his workers to seek out a medium so he could contact Samuel!

When Saul meets the psychic woman, he says: "Consult a spirit for me, and bring up for me the one whom I name to you." The medium replies (not knowing that the man in front of her is King Saul): "Surely you know what Saul has done, how he has cut off the mediums and the wizards from the land. Why then are you laying a snare for my life to bring about my death?" (Samuel 28: 8-9)

Saul's situation is not unlike church today. We are spiritually curious, yet reluctant to consult mediums, or even speak of such things in our churches. If Pastors or Ministers do consult with psychics, mediums, or healers, we do so in our private time, outside the watchful gaze of our congregants. We, like Saul, outlaw these "occult" gifts explicitly or implicitly in our churches while seeking them out for our own private benefit.

Jesus invites us to hold "occult" gifts in the same way that he invites us to hold all gifts- as blessings from God, through which we are meant to bless others. In 1 Corinthians 12, where the apostle Paul talks about the church being one body and many members, every one of us is part of the body of the Infinite. If we cause hurt by downgrading or demeaning another's God-given gifts, we hurt ourselves.

Since we are one body, any time a single body part is hurt, the entire body suffers.

Jesus invites us to a spiritual paradigm that transcends demonization, moves away from tolerance, and founds itself in the centrality of love. When we truly love another, we see God in them. To love as God does is to see God in all things, including every gift that we and others have been bestowed with. It is for this reason that Paul's next chapter in the letter to the Corinthians (the famous Chapter 13) talks about the primacy of love.

You may have the greatest gifts, Paul says, but if you don't have love, it means nothing! "If I speak with human eloquence and angelic ecstasy but don't love, I'm nothing but the creaking of a rusty gate. If I speak God's Word with power, revealing all his mysteries and making everything plain as day, and if I have faith that says to a mountain, "Jump," and it jumps, but I don't love, I'm nothing. If I give everything I own to the poor and even go to the stake to be burned as a martyr, but I don't love, I've gotten nowhere. So, no matter what I say, what I believe, and what I do, I'm bankrupt without love.[67]

The use of our gifts is bankrupt without love!

Too often, we confuse our gifts with who we are. Whether our skill be in politics, religion, science, education, sports, or elsewhere, when we let power go to our head, we forget that the power behind all these gifts is not ours, but divine. When we place our identity in "our" gifts, we get stuck in contractive ego-identification. How many people have been through a crisis of faith when their gift is taken away through injury, disease, old age, a job loss, or otherwise?

Spiritual maturity invites us to remember that all gifts are given to us by God. As such, they are best used with humility, in a spirit of selfless service. Those who thrive in their vocational lives realize the wisdom that no gift belongs to them. The gifts we hold are simply on loan from God for service to humanity. Our task is to be good stewards of these gifts.

We effectively steward our gifts when we are channels for God's love to flow through in the use of our talents and skills.

Think of a time when you were looking for help through a customer "service" representative yet felt like you received anything but service. All of us have been on the receiving end of another's lack of stewardship.

Service in its highest expression is just another form of love. As such, if our service is not infused with love, it has only the name, but lacks the essence. Service without the essence of love is spiritually

---

[67]   1 Corinthians 13: 1-7, *The Message* Translation

empty. Service infused with love is the "still more excellent way" that Paul refers to in his letter to the Corinthians[68], and that Jesus and saints of every religion model for us through the example of their lives. Let us live in that still more excellent way.

---

[68] 1 Corinthians 12: 31

ACKNOWLEDGEMENTS

To my dear friend, partner, and wife LaToya, thank you for loving me unconditionally and supporting me every step along the path. It is a joy to grow on this journey together.

To my beautiful daughter Sage- I started this book long before you were an idea in your parent's heads, and only finished this book when you were one year old. I pray that this book provides hope for the emerging future of religion and spirituality grounded in Jesus and saints of all religions. When I look into your eyes, I see the divine so clearly. I pray that as you explore spirituality for yourself, the divine spark within you only grows.

To my amazing parents, Eric and Lynn Carriker, thank you for embodying agape love in my life from a young age up until today. It is because of your formative influence that I am who I am. I am constantly inspired by your example and your love.

To family and friends too numerous to name, thank you for being there and for loving me for who I am. What a blessing.

To the Agape community, thank you for walking with me in creating this new, exciting expression of beloved community. I am inspired by your willingness to walk into unchartered territory and say "Yes" to where the Spirit is leading.

To the Presence that I sometimes call God, but that no name can capture, I am eternally grateful. Your guiding hand has been present every step along my path, and for that, I humbly bow in gratitude.

To the spiritual teachers over the years who have guided me in the path of unconditional love, thank you. You are too numerous to name. As a starting point, I offer my deepest gratitude to Paramhansa Yogananda, Swami Kriyananda, Asha Nayaswami, Nayaswamis Jyotish and Devi Novak, Mirabai Devi, Thich Nhat Hanh, Neale Donald Walsch, Henri Nouwen, Rev. Dr. Kirk Jones, Kerry Maloney, and Sister Leona Panton.

And to Jesus, the humble carpenter from Nazareth who catalyzed my spiritual journey, and who always takes me out of my comfort zone to grow more deeply into Infinite love, thank you. You are still speaking today. I pray that I continue to listen with open ears and an open heart.

ABOUT THE AUTHOR

As an ordained Christian minister in the United Church of Christ (UCC), Matt Carriker is also an author, spiritual coach, and retreat leader. Matt currently pastors a new UCC church start in Waltham, Massachusetts called "Agape Spiritual Community." Matt co-facilitates confirmation, youth, and adult spiritual formation retreats through the Southern New England Conference UCC. Matt is passionate about altering Christianity today into a spiritual tradition that models the unconditional love of God and the life and teachings of Jesus, and that engages in both contemplation and action. This is his first book. More info about "Giving Christianity Back to Agape Love" and Agape Spiritual Community can be found here:

https://www.achristianyogi.com
http://www.agapewaltham.org

CPSIA information can be obtained
at www.ICGtesting.com
Printed in the USA
BVHW081511011022
648254BV00001B/5